PRINCIPAL INDUCTION

PRINCIPAL INDUCTION

A Standards–Based

Model for

ADMINISTRATOR DEVELOPMENT

ELAINE L. WILMORE

CORWIN PRESS
A Sage Publications Company
Thousand Oaks, California

For information:

Corwin Press
A Sage Publications Company
2455 Teller Road
Thousand Oaks, California 91320
www.corwinpress.com

Sage Publications Ltd.
6 Bonhill Street
London EC2A 4PU
United Kingdom

Sage Publications India Pvt. Ltd.
B-42, Panchsheel Enclave
Post Box 4109
New Delhi 110 017 India

Printed in the United States of America

Library of Congress Cataloging-in-Publication Data

Wilmore, Elaine L.
Principal induction: A standards-based model for administrator development / Elaine L. Wilmore.
    p. cm.
Includes bibliographical references and index.
ISBN 0-7619-3868-0 (cloth)—ISBN 0-7619-3869-9 (paper)
    1. First year school principals—In-service training—United States. 2. School administrators—In-service training—United States. 3. School management and organization—Standards—United States. I. Title.
LB1738.5.W55 2004
371.2´012´07155—dc22   2003017023

This book is printed on acid-free paper.

03   04   05   06   07   10   9   8   7   6   5   4   3   2   1

Acquisitions Editor:	Robert D. Clouse
Editorial Assistant:	Jingle Vea
Production Editor:	Diane S. Foster
Copy Editor:	Elizabeth S. Budd
Typesetter:	C&M Digitals (P) Ltd.
Proofreader:	Olivia Weber
Indexer:	Molly Hall
Cover Designer:	Michael Dubowe
Graphic Designer:	Lisa Miller

Contents

Foreword

Until now, most principal induction, administrator in-service training, and assessment in the United States has been haphazard with no discrete model for improvement. With the increasing shortage and decreasing retention of quality school leaders, a more disciplined, quality theory has been desperately needed. Elaine Wilmore's *Principal Induction: A Standards-Based Model for Administrator Development* fills this need. It integrates the key national Educational Leadership Constituent Council (ELCC) standards with excellent clarifying rationale and practical uses, as well as ideas and activities to ensure the induction and retention of principals as they become more effective. The ELCC standards are the most comprehensive set for principals because they result from the work of the ten leading educational organizations interested in school leadership and improvement. In addition to the standards, this book also weaves the latest research on principal effectiveness and instructional improvement into easy-to-read narratives and case studies while providing worthwhile learning activities for prospective principals in university programs as well as for those going through induction in school districts. It focuses on active, student-centered learning. Students, school district leaders, and professors alike will find the information it provides helpful, motivating, and easy to implement. No other book of this type exists. *Principal Induction* well serves people, districts, universities, and other agencies interested in recruiting, inducting, preparing, and assessing future school principals for both formative and summative purposes. More important, it provides a model to help readers grow and succeed through increased student learning and improved school culture, climate, and vision. Thus, by improved induction and development of school leaders, we ensure greater learning for America's students and enjoy the benefits this can have on society. As research proves, a strong principal is the key to school improvement and pupil achievement. Wilmore's *Principal Induction* provides both the model and the tools that have been missing to ensure this occurs.

Principal Induction has my highest endorsement for its content, learning experiences, and ideas, and for Wilmore's unique ability to blend theory, research, standards, practice, and inspiration into a meaningful set of learning philosophies and experiences that enhance teaching and learning in each school in which it is implemented. For administrators who really want to improve their schools through their own growth and development, this is the book for them. Bravo!

Michael Martin

Associate Vice President for
Technology and Learning Innovation
University of Colorado

Preface

Principal Induction: A Standards-Based Model for Principal Development was written to focus on the critical importance of the induction process in the recruitment, development, and retention of school administrators. Never in our history has the United States experienced such a shortage of quality principals. A major indicator is that new principals, as well as assistant principals, are experiencing deep frustrations over the transition from classroom positions to the complex roles of school leadership. The structure of the job, combined with the additional stress and time demands, can wreak havoc on both new and experienced administrators, profoundly affecting their personal and family lives as well as creating problems with their health and job satisfaction. Many do not survive. They return to teaching, take early retirement, or leave education entirely. The result is that we are loosing quality people and experiencing a shortage of trained and certified school administrators.

Although new teachers experience similar problems during their induction process, there are many existing federal, state, and local resources now available to support them. Unfortunately, for school administrators, these resources are both limited and expensive. Materials are desperately needed to help administrators guide themselves through the induction process. The same materials are needed for districts, states, and education service centers to use as a centerpiece for training programs. *Principal Induction: A Standards-Based Model for Principal Development* creates a framework by which principal induction programs can be developed nationally and implemented for administrator induction, development, and retention.

Principal Induction is both unique and timely in format. It is the first to tie principal induction to the new Educational Leadership Constituent Council (ELCC) standards and is a timely follow-up to my previous book, *Principal Leadership: Applying the Educational Leadership Constituent Council Standards,* also published by Corwin Press. *Principal Leadership* remains the first and only book to tie the ELCC standards to principal preparation. In like manner, *Principal Induction* is the first to correlate the administrative induction process to these same standards. It is both distinctive and opportune in its approach of tying the new standards to practical yet research-based induction activities for principals and others interested in not only surviving during those critical early administrative years, but also flourishing. Although based on eminent leadership and management theory and research, this informative book is written in an informative, yet practical, readable, interesting, insightful, and inspiring manner. Future administrators may use it as a text for university coursework. Current administrators will use it for individual or group reflective professional development. States, districts, consultants, and education service centers can use it as a framework for planned induction programs, seminars, and conferences. However you choose to put these ideas to work, the important thing is to do just that—read and then put them to work!

Acknowledgments

My mother, Irene Watson Litchfield, went to Heaven on September 14, 2002, while I was writing this book. She was 89 years old and had lived with us for the last 6 years of her life. She was such a blessing and inspiration to our whole family and everyone else who knew her. She had strength, courage, faith, honor, and wonderful wit and wisdom. She added nothing but joy to our lives until she got that stomachache and died.

I was my mother's only child. She loved me with her whole heart. When she went to Heaven, I was holding her hand, and her eyes were on me. It was the hardest thing I have ever done in my whole life. I cannot put into words the grief and loss I still feel. I didn't just lose my mother. I lost my best friend.

So, Mama, this book's for you.

Thank you to the rest of my family—Greg, Brandon, Brooke, Brittani, and Ryan—as well as to all of my precious friends who helped me through that horrible time before I could "get my act together" to complete this project. It is also why this book is so important to me. It came straight from my heart at a time when I was hurting.

I hope that as you read it, you will read it as my mother would have . . . with great love.

For the Future,
Elaine

"Thy word is a lamp unto my feet, and a light unto my path."
Psalm 119:105

Corwin Press gratefully acknowledges the contributions of the following reviewers:

Judith Aiken
Author, Associate Professor
College of Education and
    Social Services
University of Vermont
Burlington, VT

Kermit Buckner
Professor and Chair
College of Education
East Carolina University
Greenville, NC

Helen E. R. Ditzhazy
Professor
Educational Leadership
Eastern Michigan University
Ypsilanti, MI

Sandra Harris
Assistant Professor
Department of Education &
    Educational Leadership
Stephen F. Austin State University
Nacogdoches, TX

Judith C. Houle
Assistant Professor
Educational Leadership Programs
University of Hartford
West Hartford, CT

Cathy S. Jording
Assistant Professor
College of Education
Georgia Southern University
Statesbro, GA

Beverly Kasper
Assistant Professor
School of Education
Loyola University Chicago
Chicago, IL

Michael Martin
Vice President for Technology and
    Learning Innovation
University of Colorado
Boulder, CO

Jesse Jai McNeil, Jr.
President
McNeil Educational Leadership
    Foundation
Dallas, TX

Amy Mellencamp
Principal
Burlington High School
Burlington, VT

Rosemary Papalewis
Author, Professor and Director
Center for Teaching and Learning
California State University,
    Sacramento
Sacramento, CA

James L. Pate
Assistant Professor
Educational Leadership
Valdosta State University
Valdosta, GA

Leonard O. Pellicer
Author, Dean
College of Education and
    Organizational Leadership
University of La Verne
La Verne, CA

Donald Poplau
Principal
Mankato East High School
Makato, MN

About the Author

Elaine L. Wilmore, PhD, is Special Assistant to the Dean for NCATE Accreditation and Associate Professor of Educational Leadership and Policy Studies at the University of Texas at Arlington. This year she is President of three organizations: the National Council of Professors of Educational Administration, the Cleburne (TX) Independent School District Board of Trustees, and Elaine L. Wilmore Leadership Initiatives. She is the founding Director of the University of Texas at Arlington's School of Administration Programs, Educational Leadership UTA, and the Scholars of Practice, innovative programs for which she has received extensive external grants. At the university she has served as Chair of Educational Administration and Director of University Program Development. In addition, Wilmore is active on many other local, state, and national boards, including the Texas Principals Leadership Initiative and the National Council of Professors of Educational Administration. She has served as President of the Texas Professors of Educational Administration, on the Boards of the Texas Association of School Administrators, and the Texas Consortium of Colleges of Teacher Education and was in the original cadre of program and folio reviewers for the Educational Leadership Constituent Council for NCATE. Wilmore is known in Texas as the "ExCET–TExES Queen" for her statewide success in helping students pass administrative certification examinations.

Wilmore is a former public school teacher, counselor, and elementary and middle school principal. A frequent national speaker and author, she is known for inspiring others to greatness. In addition to her significant work in the area of administrator development, she enjoys singing in her church choir, reading, writing, and spending time with those she loves. She is married and the mother of three wonderful children, one fabulous son-in-law, a big Boxer dog, and a very persistent mutt-cat named "Yum."

To my precious parents,
Lee Litchfield
February 20, 1904 – June 9, 1987
and
Irene Watson Litchfield
June 16, 1913 – September 14, 2002
I will love you both forever.

"Trust in the Lord with all your heart,
and lean not on your own understanding;
In all your ways acknowledge Him, and
He shall direct your paths."
Proverbs 3:5

"Train up a child in the way he should go, and
when he is old he will not depart from it."
Proverbs 22:6

Induction

The Big Picture

Though we travel the world over to find the beautiful, we must carry it with us or we find it not.

—Ralph Waldo Emerson

Every day we hear more stories about the shortage of good principals, the lack of quality and diversity among applicants seeking to enter the field, and the stress and heartache of those already here. We see so many others who have the potential to continue as great assets to schools who are thinking about leaving. It tears at my heart to see good people struggling to be productive as well as survive in schools that face the huge challenges of today. As society has changed, so have our schools. Students, teachers, and administrators come to school stressed and worried by myriad problems in their daily lives. For many, teaching and learning is the last thing on their minds. Just making it through the day or week is the larger problem. Life has become a rat race. People are pushed and pushing to get more done in less time than is reasonable to expect. Sooner or later, life takes its toll, and anxiety and burnout start to take over. Another good educator bites the dust. The pay is low, and the stress is high. Societal problems manifest at school. Political agendas contrary to the developmental needs of learners are apparent at both the state and federal level, and a support network to nurture and encourage educators seems to be nonexistent.

All of this is particularly true for administrators. Therefore, it is no surprise that the documented and growing shortage of quality principals continues to rise (Fenwick & Pierce, 2001; Million, 1998; Potter, 2001;

Richardson, 1999; "Study Warns," 1998; U.S. Bureau of Labor Statistics, 2000–2001). Some things must change, and that is what this book is all about.

In the midst of this blur and confusion, another generation of students comes to school. Why do they come? Some come because it is the law or because it is a family expectation. Others come because the school is the one safe place they know where they can be warm in the winter, cool in the heat, and get a decent meal. Others come for social reasons. They want to see their friends. Others come because there is just no other place to go. Then there are many who come, but don't really want to.

When they get here, there are those who want to learn. Others don't begin to care. Some create a ruckus because any attention from the teacher or their peers beats no attention at all. Some students are bright and motivated. Others are bright, but not motivated at all. Others are not so bright, have learning difficulties, or are simply bored. Who knows? It is easy to conclude that not every student comes to school with an undying desire to learn—simply for the sake of acquiring knowledge. It is also safe to say that not all educators show up with a burning desire to make a difference in the lives of every student with whom they come in contact throughout the day. Time, repetition, and life have turned many motivated educators into perfunctory delivers of knowledge instead of interested and stimulating developers of young people.

THE BANDWAGON

My students often call me Pollyanna the Idealist. I correct them and say I am a pragmatist who wants to change the world one school at a time. Then I ask them to come help me. They grin. I can almost hear them thinking, "That's our Dr. Wilmore. She's on a bandwagon all the time." I smile silently to myself because by the end of the semester, they are encouraging others to join us in our crusade to make our schools and society a better place.

That's what this book is all about. It's the bandwagon for us all to join as we develop strategies and ways to support principals in the field. This book is particularly designed to help new administrators as they attempt to sail the hurricane-force winds of their induction years in the principalship. It is about providing them with multiple mentors who have a specific induction plan to support yet will prod new leaders to professional and personal excellence (see Figure 1.1).

But this book is not just for new principals. This book is for all of us who together want to make a difference in schools that will manifest itself

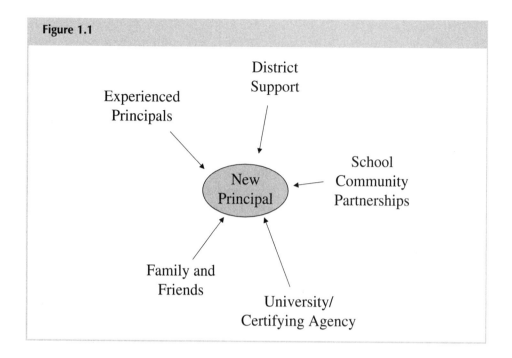

Figure 1.1

through increased student learning, a better economy for all families, social justice and equity, and a better, more democratic society for everyone. We cannot have schools that are led by qualified, diverse leaders if they quit, burn out, or die while trying to survive the storms. They have got to have some help. Even principals who have been successful for years need a place to rejuvenate and prepare to face the challenges of each new day. This model will do that for each of them.

THE COAST GUARD HAS ARRIVED

That's where this book comes in for you and me. Together we will learn about the standards-based Induction Partnership Model for Administrator Development. Together we are the Coast Guard coming to the rescue. We're here to help. Put on your life jacket because we just arrived. It's time for all of us to go make a difference, one school at a time (Wilmore, 2001), beginning with our novices. If they do not survive these first few years, they cannot effect true and lasting change in the lives, histories, and legacies of schools and society. It is not someone else's job. It is our job. If we don't do it, it won't get done. Won't you come along with us?

From a different perspective, this book is also for the seasoned veterans who want to be of help to new administrators but really don't know how.

It's for the existing administrators, university professors, and community leaders who want to be a part of positive change, of making schools better, and of becoming empowered in the process. This book has something for everyone, from the new principal; to the wise and experienced veteran; to those in the field who have been there, done that, and burnt out; to business and community leaders, central office administrators, school board members, and state and federal departments of education. It is time for all the various groups with varying ideas, policies, and philosophies to come together for a common cause. As shown in Figure 1.2, it is time to nurture, groom, and develop each other so we all can become everything we have the potential of being. It is a growth process aimed at improving schools by enhancing the human and leadership qualities of their administrators.

Research has long validated the single most important characteristic of effective schools is their principal. Forget Democrat, Republican, or Green Party. Forget vouchers or charters. Let's form our own party, the For the Future Party, and create partnerships with high ideals. For our time together in this book, let's focus on improving *every* school for *every* student by cultivating *every* principal. Let's not leave our people out there to drown in the storm. The Coast Guard is here, and it is you and me. Let's go get 'em.

INDUCTION

Webster defines induction as "the act or process of inducting (as into office)" or "an initial experience" (Agnes, 2001). Principal induction fits both descriptions. Beginning administrators are experiencing an initial reaction in the journey of becoming school leaders. Most new administrators are already successful teachers, but even the most seasoned of veterans experience culture shock when they leave the classroom and take on the responsibilities of assistant principalships or, in some cases, becoming the actual principal. That's where the rude awakening sets in. No matter how good their internship has been, unless it was a long-term, daily experience in which the inductee actually performed the job full time in a university–school collaborative partnership, it is natural to feel overwhelmed during the transition. Even under the best of circumstances, induction is difficult.

Often the difficulty lasts long after the induction. We've all seen beginning and experienced administrators who have that "deer in the headlights" look as reality hits. New administrators who are so motivated to create change and do the right things—fairly and ethically—to help teachers teach and students learn confront the cold, hard reality of the

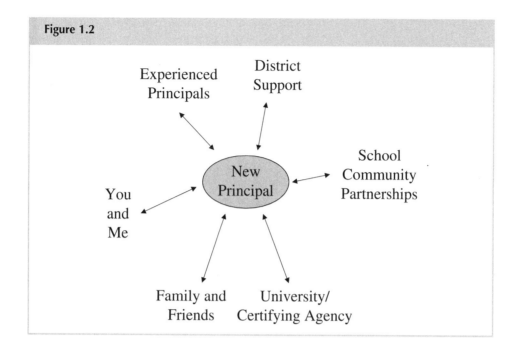

Figure 1.2

real-world, day-to-day workplace. Eventually they can lose sight of their passion and of their vision of excellence. Some become what they least wanted to be: They become status quo principals. They manage, but they do not lead their schools. They take care of the daily operations, organization, and resources but rarely take risks for school improvement. Although risk taking is creative and challenging, it can be problematic because not every risk is successful. That's why they call it "risk taking." These principals have become complacent and content in their status quo world and do not want to risk failure, even if the possibility of great reward is a possible outcome. In their minds, having a status quo school that is not in the headlines beats the alternative. Gambling with change is not worth the effort.

Sooner or later, all leaders learn the age-old adage, "It's lonely at the top." From the most thick-skinned to the most sensitive, each internalizes experiences differently. While some seem to be able to tolerate the stress more than others, when being most honest all would admit that the transition to administration is a scary process. When it stops being scary, you aren't taking the job seriously enough. The future of the United States, of society as we know it, and of democracy itself, is in the hands of the school children we serve. Yes, it is a frightening responsibility throughout your career. If it weren't, you'd have become a status quo principal. Either participate in rejuvenating, "stewardship of the vision" developmental activities or quit. Wal-Mart is hiring. Get a job there, or anywhere outside of education for that matter. Our schools' welfare and productivity is much too important to be led by those who are not fully committed to making a difference. Just showing up every day, going through the motions, and doing the right things is not enough. True leaders have a passion and commitment that will not let anything stop them as they search for new ways to meet the needs of all students. That is what school leadership is all about. Anything else will simply not do.

EDUCATIONAL LEADERSHIP CONSTITUENT COUNCIL STANDARDS

In this book, we will look at the induction process—who can and should be involved and for what reasons. We will study the standards-based Induction Partnership Model to see what it is, how it works, and for what purposes. We will tie the reality of practicality to the theory and research analyzed and synthesized by the Educational Leadership Constituent Council (ELCC) into the seven leadership standards used today for principal preparation and, in our case, development. The ELCC is the arm of the National Council for the Accreditation of Teacher Education (NCATE) charged with the process of preparing and developing school leaders. These new standards are a joint effort of several professional organizations that focus on improved administrator preparation, development, and standards (Council of Chief State School Officers, 1996; Murphy & Shipman, 1998; Murphy, Shipman, & Pearlman, 1997; Murphy, Yff, & Shipman, 2000; National Policy Board for Educational Administration, 2001; Thomson, 1993; Van Meter & Murphy, 1997). These organizations include NCATE, the National Policy Board for Educational Administration, the Interstate School Leaders Licensure Consortium (ISLLC), and each of their many member organizations. The purpose of the standards is to improve principal preparation programs and to serve as a framework for current administrators' professional development. Until this set of standards was adopted in 2002, preparation programs and districts providing developmental activities were faced with the cumbersome task of trying to address two sets of often-overlapping standards simultaneously. Through an extensive and time-consuming process, the original ISLLC and ELCC standards were synthesized into these new ELCC standards around which this induction model is built. Let's read them now as an overview. Chapters 3 through 9 will develop the standards fully and tie them to the Induction Partnership Model.

THE STANDARDS

It is a rare thing indeed when multiple professional organizations can debate, analyze, and finally reach consensus on one set of principal standards. This is what has occurred with the new Educational Leadership Constituent Council standards and what makes them the premier set of principles on which significant national work is being developed. They are also the framework used here for the Induction Partnership Model. The standards are as follows.

Standard 1

Candidates who complete the program are educational leaders who have the knowledge and ability to promote the success of all students by facilitating the development, articulation, implementation, and stewardship of a school or district vision of learning supported by the school community.

Standard 2

Candidates who complete the program are educational leaders who have the knowledge and ability to promote the success of all students by promoting a positive school culture, providing an effective instructional program, applying best practice to student learning, and designing comprehensive professional growth plans for staff.

Standard 3

Candidates who complete the program are educational leaders who have the knowledge and ability to promote the success of all students by managing the organization, operations, and resources in a way that promotes a safe, efficient, and effective learning environment.

Standard 4

Candidates who complete the program are educational leaders who have the knowledge and ability to promote the success of all students by collaborating with families and other community members, responding to diverse community interests and needs, and mobilizing community resources.

Standard 5

Candidates who complete the program are educational leaders who have the knowledge and ability to promote the success of all students by acting with integrity, fairly, and in an ethical manner.

Standard 6

Candidates who complete the program are educational leaders who have the knowledge and ability to promote the success of all students by understanding, responding to, and influencing the larger political, social, economic, legal, and cultural context.

Standard 7

The internship provides significant opportunities for candidates to synthesize and apply the knowledge and practice and develop the skills identified in Standards 1–6 through substantial, sustained, standards-based work in real settings, planned and guided cooperatively by the institution, and school district personnel for graduate credit.

In our case we are concerned with candidates studying to become principals, with new administrators, and with current practicing principals who need a shot in the arm to refocus on their personal stewardship of the vision. It is a tall ambition, but with focus, determination, commitment, and sheer grit, we will get it done.

ALL SET?

We have discussed the need for an induction process that supports and nurtures both beginning and existing school leaders. The standards-based Induction Partnership Model that we will analyze and apply here will provide the framework for a multiple "win-win" process (see Figure 1.2, page 5). Each person involved will grow. The Induction Partnership Model is a true collaborative with multiple stakeholders involved in creating mutual growth for everyone. Although the focus is on the mentee, attention is paid to all partners. A partnership does not consist of a single person. A partnership by definition involves more than one person, group, or organization. Chapter 2 describes the background and components of the Induction Partnership Model, defines the roles and responsibilities of each stakeholder, and describes what's in it for you.

2 The Partnership Model for Administrator Induction Success

Nothing contributes so much to tranquilizing the mind as a steady purpose—a point on which the soul may fix its intellectual eye.

—Mary Wollstonecraft Shelley

As we know, there is a critical and growing shortage of quality teachers (Clinton, 2003; Snyder, 2001; U.S. Department of Education, 2002; Whitehurst, 2002; Wise, 2002) and principals (McCowan, Arnold, Miles, & Hargadine, 2000; Medina, 2003; National Association of Elementary School Principals, n.d.; National Association of Secondary School Principals, 2002, 2003; Schnur, 2002; Snyder, 2001) across the United States. A longitudinal study investigating the reasons teachers and principals leave the profession is called for in an attempt to uncover potential solutions. Qualitative evidence continually points to such issues as changes in society, lack of respect from students and parents, poor discipline, increasing demands for extra time spent outside of school hours, stress, high-stakes testing, and low salaries (Keeton Strayhorn, 2003; Snyder, 2001; Wise, 2002). If these factors are addressed, a serious step toward keeping experienced educators in the field will occur, improving student performance and saving vast resources on recruitment, training, and retention.

BACKGROUND CHECK

Mentoring has long been known to be a critical element in the development of leaders in all organizations (Bolman & Deal, 2002; Maxwell, 1995; Portner, 2002). Various forms of teacher mentoring have been implemented in multiple districts, with various results. Recent developments in the area of teacher mentoring for maximum effectiveness and retention have shown promise. Although concerns about the administrator shortage are more recent, there have been fewer resources devoted to the development and job satisfaction levels of both new principals entering the field and experienced ones who are experiencing frustrations or burnout. The Management Profile, developed and implemented through the Principals' Center at Texas A&M University under the direction of David Erlandson, is one such model (Erlandson, Atkinson, & Wilmore, 1995; Erlandson, Lacy, & Wilmore, 1990; Wilmore, 1988, 1992, 1993; Wilmore & Atkinson, 1993; Wilmore & Erlandson, 1993). The Management Profile was developed through research sponsored by the National Commission on Standards for the Principalship and the National Association of Secondary School Principals. Based on videotaped interviews of administrators and scored along performance criteria, principals wrote professional development plans designed to utilize their strengths to improve their weaknesses. Although effective, the Management Profile was also time consuming and lacked continuous mentee feedback or an accountability system. The Induction Partnership Model is based, in large part, on gleanings learned from research through the Management Profile.

STANDARDS BASED

Throughout efforts toward standards-based change in our schools, common problems have been lack of consistent follow-up, lack of a reliable accountability system, burdensome time constraints, and conflicts with other commitments. Administrators desperately need the knowledge and skills necessary to support changing societal issues, norms, diversity, and the impact of poverty on student learning. The Induction Partnership Model is designed to address each of these issues by connecting administrator development to the Educational Leadership Constituent Council standards (Wilmore, 2000) in a user-friendly, structured, and productive manner (Figure 2.1).

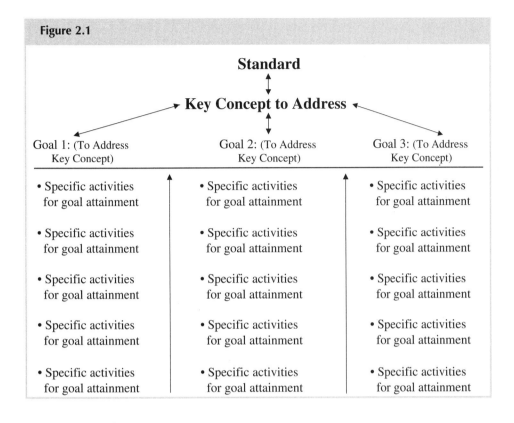

Figure 2.1

Taken in totality, the standards cover the full range of essential administrator knowledge and skills. Each standard is discussed in detail in Chapters 3 through 9. Knowing the particular insecurities of new administrators as well as the huge responsibilities they are undertaking, it is obvious that they need and deserve a support system. The utilization of the Standards-Based Induction Partnership Model allows a team of selected individuals help the new administrator target growth needs through the ELCC standards as a basic framework. As shown in Figure 2.1, identified goals are mutually developed to help the mentee grow in the targeted area. Subsequent developmental activities are then designed to facilitate the mentee to achieve the targeted goal to help him or her mature toward the identified key concept and standard. The exact number of goals and activities to attain the goal is up to the individual team. Individual mentees will have different areas in which they need further enhancement. Obviously, some standards will need more attention and time than others, but the main idea is to work together as a team to determine where the most attention is needed, to develop goals to help the mentee grow, to identify specific activities for goal attainment, and to determine how success will be measured.

The fictional story of the potential impact of a single mentor on a new principal is powerfully described in Bolman and Deal's (2002) *Reframing the Path to School Leadership*. Multiple real-life stories of similar benefits have been told repeatedly. Combining those experiences with the impact of the Management Profile and adding the powerful, value-added factors of multiple mentors and an accountability system with specific time lines, the Induction Partnership Model is able to provide support, specific guidance, developmental activities, and the commitment of many partners. With a situation like that, how can you lose?

THE INDUCTION PARTNERSHIP MODEL

The Induction Partnership Model is based on the Stephen Covey philosophy of creating a "win-win" situation (1990a, 1990b). It encompasses multiple stakeholders including the mentee; a specifically selected mentor who has agreed to serve; the district, the university or other certifying agency; business and school community partners; as well as family and selected friends of the administrator. By involving so many parties with mutual interests, commitment, and accountability, a true "win-win" situation develops.

Everyone wins. When the partners invest in the mentee, each of them grows, learns, and develops proportionately. This is explained and understood when they *agree* to participate. With each entity invested in the principal's success, everyone benefits. People support what they help to create. Because team members were individually selected, had their responsibilities spelled out to them, and were asked to participate, they understand and accept their responsibilities when they agree to be involved. They have ownership in it. Then, because the input and output vary for each team, stakeholders create their own structures, set their own goals, and develop their own accountability system and time lines. It is theirs. It belongs to them. Therefore, they structure the team the way they want. This, coupled with voluntary participation, creates an intrinsic investment in the mentee's achievement. With each of these diverse stakeholders collaboratively working toward the growth of the mentee, success is inevitable. When the entire Induction Partnership team wins, students, faculty, families, and the school community win as well. What more can we ask?

HOW DOES IT WORK?

The Induction Partnership Model is a predictor to administrator success because it is based on common sense and practicality. All administrators, as well as team members, are busy people. They are all asked to do too many things. Therefore, the sage rule of "keep it simple, stupid" is enforced. For people to stick with a project, it must make sense, be easy to use, not be unduly time-consuming, and be focused on improving administrator and school performance. The team members are interested in working together as a team to make certain its goals are achieved.

The process of developing and implementing an Induction Partnership team is also easy. Any administrator, whether new or experienced, can put it to use. First, administrators take time to jot down the names of people they respect, and with whom they feel comfortable; the result is a list of people to consider asking to be a part of the team. The list of people must comprise the following:

- A specific *mentor* who is an experienced administrator. (The mentor does not have to be within the same school or even the same district as the montee, but the person selected should be someone the mentee respects and to whom he or she has regular access; the person should be easy to communicate with and must *agree* to serve rather than be *required* to serve.)
- A *district* representative, probably from the upper administrative level, who is committed to helping the mentee develop and who will incorporate the district's global perspective.
- A *university or certifying agency* representative who will help connect the theoretical concepts gained in the learning and certifying process to the reality of school leadership.
- A *business-school community* representative who will bring grassroots views to ensure the team stays grounded in community needs, concerns, and school improvement from the citizen's perspective.
- *Family and friends.*

In particular, family and friends are included on the team because none among us can truly separate our professional and personal lives. It's impossible. Those closest to us are the ones in whom we confide, bearing our hearts and souls. Of course, they have an interest in anything that makes our lives better. They want to help us but often don't know how. By bringing them into the circle, we involve them in the process and give them the tools to help. As important as anything else is the vast, intangible asset of having people who truly care about your welfare on your team.

Sometimes, when an administrator identifies and asks people from each of these groups to be a part of his or her Induction Partnership team, those selected express reservations about serving. Although they are usually honored that the new administrator thinks so highly of them, potential team members can be daunted with concerns such as the following:

- Do I know enough to mentor someone else?
- How much time will it take?
- How and where will we meet?
- Who else will be on the team?
- Why should I be crazy enough to commit to something like this?

At this point, the administrator should carefully remind the potential team member that one of the strengths of the Induction Partnership Model is the collaborative culture on which it is built. A key component to being a good mentor is caring about the mentee. Remind potential team members that if they care about you and your administrative development, that is all the training they need. Mentoring should occur in a familial, supportive manner; the sole purpose is to help someone else succeed on his or her own terms. The climate of the team must be conducive to providing a strongly supportive environment. For this reason, the team should comprise people who have mutual respect for the mentee and the Induction Partnership process. The amount of time necessary will vary from mentee to mentee and situation to situation. During stressful times, the team may meet more often than when things are going smoothly, but generally team members must determine together their preference for how often to have regularly scheduled meetings, where these will occur, and at what time of day. Some teams may prefer to meet for breakfast. Others may prefer evenings or weekends. It makes no difference. Meeting times reflect the individual schedules of the participants. The ultimate goal is to have a schedule and to keep to it as much as possible. In addition, team members should be flexible about adding or changing times, locations, scenarios, goals, targeted activities, time lines, and assessment mechanisms.

FROM MODEL TO REALITY

Now that we know the basic parameters of the model, let's discuss the Three Point Plan for getting things going.

Point 1: Prework

The team selection process is the initial step of the model. When constructing a team, remember to consider the interdynamics of the people involved. It will not help the mentee if the team members are great and highly respected but simply do not work well together for whatever reason. The combination of people should be able to create a culture, climate, and vision for the group that centers on mentee growth and development for the purpose of improved student learning and organizational productivity. The mentee can select additional criteria to address specific things that he or she thinks will be helpful to the team process. The selection process is critical to the success of the model, so be sure to give this careful consideration.

Point 2: Initial Meeting

Once the team is identified and has accepted this developmental opportunity, members attend an informal initial meeting to get to know each other, talk about their purpose, and determine what they want to accomplish. For example, the mentee will provide an overview of the background and experiences that have brought him or her to this position; the mentee should then describe his or her greatest concerns. A team facilitator or chair should be selected for organizational purposes and to keep the team focused. The team facilitator should be selected collaboratively as the "point person" to keep things moving; this team member is the primary contact person for the mentee. From there, the process will vary from team to team according to individual goals. Structures each team will discuss should include the following:

- The team discusses the ELCC standards that provide the framework for the Induction Partnership Model.
- The mentee talks informally about joys, concerns, and frustrations with regard to his or her preparation for the principalship; the mentee also discusses what is taking place at school as well as various challenges.
- The team begins an initial discussion, connecting the issues the mentee described to the appropriate standards.
- The team brainstorms ways the team can facilitate growth for the mentee and potential goals of the process.
- The team discusses the merits or potential drawbacks of various tools for administrator development.
- The team designs a 360-degree feedback tool that directly targets potential mentee strengths and weaknesses.
- The team determines preliminary resources that will be needed.
- The team determines benchmarks for mentee success.

- The team develops cross-checks as a backbone of the model that hold each team member accountable for his or her input and responsibilities.
- The team creates an accountability system of ongoing, cyclical assessment, modification, and refinement to plans and projects for the purpose of continuous renewal and growth for all stakeholders.
- The team develops a preliminary time line of meetings that will meet each team member's schedule. This will vary from team to team, and there is no required number of meetings. This is an issue of quality versus quantity.
- The exact date, time, and location of the next meeting should be determined before the initial meeting is over.

Point 3: "Houston, We Have Liftoff!"

Utilizing the perspectives of each stakeholder, a series of meetings are undertaken over an extended period of time. The process must be long term to ensure change, growth, and reflection for each stakeholder. Throughout the process, each stakeholder will support all other stakeholders, respect the diverse perspectives of each member, and keep the focus on helping the mentee develop knowledge, skills, dispositions, and wisdom for the singular purpose of increasing PreK–12 student success. The whole experience is greater than the sum of its parts. Basic guiding questions of the team should regularly include the following:

- How can we assist the mentee in things that are occurring on his or her school right now as well as long term?
- How can we help the mentee to enhance his or her leadership capabilities?
- What impact can the outcomes of what we are doing have on student performance?
- What impact can these outcomes have on the school, the community, and society in general?

Both short- and long-term results are achieved through collaborative planning, communication, implementation of team ideas and projects, and targeted, continuous assessment with time lines. Goals without deadlines are only dreams. Administrators who have gone to all the effort to seek out and put into effect Induction Partnership teams are not dreaming. They are doing this for a reason. They *want* to grow and improve. They have asked the help of others to accomplish this. Therefore, setting time lines and deadlines is important to keeping the process moving (Figure 2.2).

Figure 2.2

Per Goal	Mentee/Self	Mentor	District	Business-School Community Partnerships	University/ Certifying Unit	Family & Friends
● Developmental Strategy						
● Resources Needed						
● Deadline						
● Desired Outcome(s)						
● As measured by						

It is critical to the success of the model that every meeting have a specific focus. Meetings should not be held for the sake of saying you had a meeting. That is how too many mentoring processes fall apart. We want this one to succeed. For that to happen, the importance of each person's individual life and other responsibilities must be considered. Don't waste time. At the end of each meeting decide together what should be accomplished before the next meeting and each person's responsibilities, including the mentee's, to guarantee that these things occur. Each team member must make a commitment before joining the team that he or she will fulfill their responsibilities on time. How can we propagate professionalism in a mentee if we do not display it ourselves?

One additional component that is vital to the success of the model is assessment. Just as administrators must continuously assess school and district programs, projects, personnel, and policies for formative and summative clarification and modification, the same is true in the Induction Partnership Model. Every meeting should include time for assessment, critical thinking, accountability, and reflection on what is being done and how it can be improved. Just because a team started in one direction does not mean it can't change as the context of the situation changes or if current strategies simply aren't successful. There is no point trying to ride a dead horse. Reassess the situation. Regroup and try new things. Time spent on things that are not working is not productive. The mentee, as well as the team, the school, and the community, do not have time for that. Fix it. Figures 2.3 through 2.8 provide examples of worksheets that can be used to ensure that each stakeholder has a clear understanding of his or her roles, time lines, and accountability. These can be modified to meet the individual needs of each team.

POTENTIAL PITFALLS

It is important to remember that any good idea can run into obstacles. The Induction Partnership Model is no exception. Here are some potential

(Continued on page 21)

Figure 2.3

To facilitate personal success, the mentee will . . .
Strategy 1:
　　By what date?_____
　　Accountability System: _____
　　_____

Strategy 2:
　　By what date?_____
　　Accountability System: _____
　　_____

Strategy 3:
　　By what date?_____
　　Accountability System: _____
　　_____

Strategy 4:
　　By what date?_____
　　Accountability System: _____
　　_____

Strategy 5:
　　By what date?_____
　　Accountability System: _____
　　_____

Figure 2.4

To facilitate success of the administrator, the mentor will . . .

Strategy 1:

By what date?_____

Accountability System: _____

_____

Strategy 2:

By what date?_____

Accountability System: _____

_____

Strategy 3:

By what date?_____

Accountability System: _____

_____

Strategy 4:

By what date?_____

Accountability System: _____

_____

Strategy 5:

By what date?_____

Accountability System: _____

_____

Figure 2.5

To facilitate success of the administrator, the district will . . .

Strategy 1:

By what date?_____

Accountability System: _____

_____

Strategy 2:

By what date?_____

Accountability System: _____

_____

Strategy 3:

By what date?_____

Accountability System: _____

_____

Strategy 4:

By what date?_____

Accountability System: _____

_____

Strategy 5:

By what date?_____

Accountability System: _____

_____

Figure 2.6

To facilitate success of the administrator, the school/community will . . .

Strategy 1:
    By what date?_____
    Accountability System: _____
    _____

Strategy 2:
    By what date?_____
    Accountability System: _____
    _____

Strategy 3:
    By what date?_____
    Accountability System: _____
    _____

Strategy 4:
    By what date?_____
    Accountability System: _____
    _____

Strategy 5:
    By what date?_____
    Accountability System: _____
    _____

Figure 2.7

To facilitate success of the administrator, the university certifying agency will . . .

Strategy 1:
    By what date?_____
    Accountability System: _____
    _____

Strategy 2:
    By what date?_____
    Accountability System: _____
    _____

Strategy 3:
    By what date?_____
    Accountability System: _____
    _____

Strategy 4:
    By what date?_____
    Accountability System: _____
    _____

Strategy 5:
    By what date?_____
    Accountability System: _____
    _____

Figure 2.8

To facilitate success of the administrator, the family and friends will . . .
   Strategy 1:
      By what date?_____
      Accountability System:_____
      _____

   Strategy 2:
      By what date?_____
      Accountability System:_____
      _____

   Strategy 3:
      By what date?_____
      Accountability System:_____
      _____

   Strategy 4:
      By what date?_____
      Accountability System:_____
      _____

   Strategy 5:
      By what date?_____
      Accountability System:_____
      _____

pitfalls your team may encounter. Being prepared for them ahead of time will help you avoid them.

Hectic Schedules: Set firm dates, times, and locations of meetings and stick to them.

Lack of Team Member Responsibility and Follow-Through: To avoid this, be proactive. As team members are selected, talk to them about time and other commitments. Get their commitment to the project ahead of time so there are no surprises later. Because they will be involved with the actual creation and initiation of this particular professional development plan, they will have ownership in it; they'll only have themselves to blame if they lose interest. Shame on them!

Loss of Mentee Commitment: This can be caused by a number of factors. If a team ever senses the mentee is losing interest, it's time to take action. Get together with the mentee and have a "tough love" accountability session. See what factors are playing into the situation and how they can be resolved in a positive manner.

In-Name-Only Support: This occurs if a district, university, certifying agency, or any other partner gives support in name only but does not come through with the promised resources. In a professional manner, the team facilitator or other member needs to address the problem so it can be resolved and productivity will continue.

Bad Meetings: Bad meetings can occur in any organization. They are unproductive or have a lack of depth that results in group dysfunction, frustration, despair, and lack of mentee–mentor growth. Bad meetings result when planning, ongoing assessment and refinement, and accountability are lacking. With these factors in place, there will be no bad meetings.

THE POWER OF PERSISTENCE

At times you will be tempted to give up. There is a shortage of time and an abundance of things to do. But don't give up. There is power in the diversity of the team, and we need that power to help others, as well as ourselves, to grow. Remember the story of Abraham Lincoln. He was not from a wealthy family, and his mother died when he was quite young. These were not ideal circumstances for a man who later changed the course of history as president of the United States during the most divisive time in our history. So what did this man with a humble education, who lost early elections to other offices, possess that had such a profound impact on American lives?

Persistence. Abraham Lincoln had persistence. Persistence is not something that can be bought or sold. It is a skill, a talent that is the difference between winners and losers. It is the ingredient for success, the requirement to ensure that principals, superintendents, and all other leaders stick with their vision and never give up. Abraham Lincoln had that grit, that faith, and that determination. In essence, he had long-term persistence to make his vision a reality. The question becomes, do we?

CONCLUSIONS

The Induction Partnership Model is an instrument that provides structured flexibility to help improve schools and society through improved administrator development. By utilizing the model to tie the research-based ELCC standards to the real world, it is the optimal tool to enhance administrator growth and professional development.

Throughout Chapters 3 through 9, each of the standards is explained in great detail with examples of principal performance for each. Problem-based case studies are provided with reflective questions that can be used for individual or group discussion, discourse, reflection, and school improvement. Each chapter also provides an application segment of the Induction Partnership Model that provides readers with the opportunity to connect the basic premises of the model with reality through the ELCC standards. Adding to the research base, each chapter provides a section of "Top Ten Things Administrators Wish They Had Known Before Entering the Principalship," as well as a section of "Sweet 16" Standards-Based Induction Developmental Activities that teams can use or modify for the benefit of improved administrator development. These were compiled from research conducted with administrators in the Dallas–Fort Worth, Texas, metropolitan area. The "Top Ten" can be used by administrator preparatory programs and coupled with the "Sweet 16" for ongoing principal development.

In the end, the true power of the model lies in the selection of team members. As noted earlier, mentees should include only team members whom they respect and with whom they are comfortable. Team members must agree to the roles and responsibilities delegated to them. By accepting these roles and responsibilities, each member is empowered and committed to the process. Although there are multiple benefits to the team members, including their own growth and the opportunity to provide leadership to others, their first focus is to help the mentee become all he or she can be, and ultimately improve student performance. Are you ready? Let's study the intricacies of each ELCC standard.

3 How Do You Stay Focused on the School Vision When the Walls Are Falling Down?

Where there is no vision the people perish.

—Proverbs 29:18

STANDARD 1

Candidates who complete the program are educational leaders with the knowledge and ability to promote the success of all students by facilitating the development, articulation, implementation, and stewardship of a school or district vision of learning, supported by the school community.

TOP TEN THINGS
ADMINISTRATORS WISH THEY HAD
KNOWN BEFORE ENTERING THE PRINCIPALSHIP

Principals must

1. Clearly understand what a school vision is before being able to lead a school to develop one.

2. Never lose sight of the school vision of excellence.

3. Understand and be able to communicate the importance of school goal setting.

4. Always focus on student needs and their best interests instead of what is easy or popular.

5. Identify and facilitate empowerment of "power base" faculty, parents, and community members with and through the school vision.

6. Involve community members in school activities and decision making as much as possible.

7. Meet with all shareholders (e.g., teachers, staff, other educators, custodians, bus drivers, cafeteria workers, etc.) on a regular basis so they can understand, be able to articulate and participate in, the school's mission and vision.

8. Evaluate everything the school and those in it, including the principal, do.

9. Learn to cope with and manage stress.

10. Appreciate and acknowledge the efforts of all stakeholders.

PHILOSOPHICAL FRAMEWORK

From the time she was a little girl, Sarah Hughes dreamed of becoming an Olympic figure skater. Throughout her childhood years, Sarah was up early practicing her skating, going to school, making excellent grades, then practicing her skating again in the evenings. This was her schedule—day after day, weekend after weekend, and year after year. During those early formative times of practicing, competitions, triumphs, and defeats, Sarah's character was also developing. Her dream was no longer to become an Olympic figure skater. It had evolved into a new goal: to win the Olympic gold medal.

As the 2002 Olympics approached, Sarah worked harder and harder toward her personal vision of excellence. She had never beaten favorite Michelle Kwan in a major competition. Further, her teammate Sasha Cohen, as well as Russia's Irina Slutskaya and other world-class skaters, were tremendous talents as well. Yet Sarah did not look at the situation as a glass half empty, but as a glass half full. She was determined to go forth, skate her best, and win.

After the short program, things did not look promising. Sarah was in fourth place behind Kwan, Slutskaya, and Cohen, but the long program carried a greater weight than the short one. Instead of giving in to disappointment and high stress, Sarah did not give up. She gave the skating performance of her life, holding nothing back, and was rewarded with the Olympic gold medal. No one that saw her shock, awe, and absolute delight that night will ever forget the face of a beautiful young woman totally blown away by the realization of her vision. Sarah's dogged hard work, dreams, aches, pains, and perseverance had paid off. She had achieved her goal, and it obviously felt so very good.

The story of Sarah Hughes is one from which all of us in leadership positions can learn. How often we see our schools the way they are instead of the way they can be. We forget to stop and really think what our own visions of excellence should be as we go through the busy details of everyday school leadership. Sarah knows something we all must also know. Her perseverance, grit, and attitude paid off. That gold medal didn't just fall in her lap. The other skaters just didn't roll over and play dead. They all did an excellent job.

Sarah won, and we want our schools to win. To help them do so, we must have a collaboratively developed vision of excellence. We have to determine together exactly what the ideal is for our individual schools for this moment in time, determine the things we will have to do to get from the way we are to the way we want to be, identify and procure the resources we need to make those things happen, then roll up our sleeves, get busy, and make it happen (Figure 3.1).

We cannot give up, rationalize, or settle for excuses. Sarah didn't give up when she was in fourth place after the short program. Yet she is a smart girl. She knew the mathematical odds of her winning a medal at all, much less the gold, were virtually nonexistent. But she did not give up. Neither can we.

This perseverance challenge is particularly difficult for new principals as they struggle to learn how to develop, articulate, implement, and steward a vision of excellence for all students while also promoting parents and other citizens to share, support, and be involved with it. Talk about multitasking! This is where idealism meets reality with a big, hard thud. Administrators can come into a new job with high hopes and expectations for a wonderful school vision. Then the cold, hard world of reality hits them square in the face as they realize that having a vision and being able to implement and steward it are two very different things.

Development of a Vision

A school vision is the all-encompassing umbrella that embraces everything the school wants to be. It is the philosophical framework on which

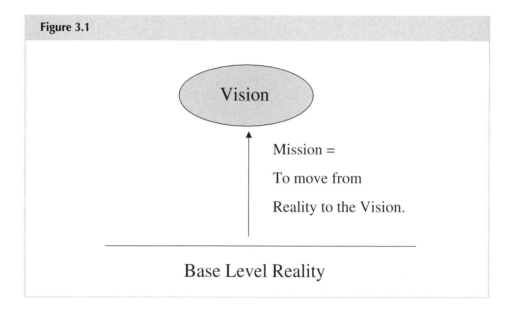

Figure 3.1

Vision

Mission =

To move from

Reality to the Vision.

Base Level Reality

school improvement and action planning are linked. The concept of an organizational or school vision is abstract and difficult for many to understand. A vision is not the same thing as a mission. The *vision* is the big or global picture of where the school wants to be, not where it actually is. That's called *reality*. The *mission* of the school is to take it from where it is to where it wants to be.

So where exactly does the school want to be and how on earth do you develop a mission, you ask? Isn't it good enough to say the vision of a school is that all students can and will learn? Well, not exactly. Let's dig a little deeper and explore how and in what ways the students can and will learn. The basic tool in making that determination is both simple and difficult. It is to communicate. It is the role of the principal to get all sorts of stakeholders talking to each other, determining by researching and analyzing school and student performance data exactly where the school is, then collaboratively deciding what they want their students to look like and be as a result of being at their school. It is more than the basic academic knowledge and skills we want them to have, but the dispositions they need to become productive citizens as identified in the school vision. This is accomplished through multiple discussions and discourse in small and large groups over a period of time, not after school one Wednesday when everyone is tired and wants to go home. There must be interactive conversations that bring together teachers, staff, auxiliary personnel, parents, and other members of the school community to share perspectives and ideas, thoroughly analyzing concepts while developing a team approach to synthesize divergent viewpoints into a common set of core values that everyone can support.

For the process to have true meaning, the school leadership team (i.e., the principal and others highly involved in decision making) must emphasize it. By simply calling a meeting and telling teachers, "Look, we've got to come up with this vision statement for the superintendent. The quicker we can get it done, the quicker we can all go home," is not going to get it done. This behavior shows the principal has no true investment in the importance of the process or its outcomes. For it to have this importance, the process must take place over time with the active involvement of teachers, staff, parents, and other community members interested in the success of the school. Time must be provided for reflective questioning, discussion, research, and analysis of student and school performance data from various sources, as well as time to let everything sink in and come together in our minds, before decisions can be made. The school vision should encompass a synthesis of the goals that stakeholders have for the knowledge, skills, and dispositions they want students to possess by having been a part of their learning community. When this is done collaboratively, all the stakeholders will support it because people support what they help create.

Once the vision has been developed by a diverse team of stakeholders, there's more work to do. The vision is only the first step toward the development of an ongoing School Improvement Plan, which has somehow developed a bad rap because of its having been overdeveloped and underutilized. The key to school improvement is great thought and simple structures. To that end, let's see what to do next.

Once the vision has been developed, specific targeted goals must be identified that will facilitate the school, grade, or content area reaching the vision. In other words, there should not be any goals for any school that are not there for the purpose of helping the school obtain its vision (Figure 3.2). In fact, absolutely nothing should take place in schools that does not help them reach their vision. If something does not do that, it is a waste of time. We do not have enough time to fool around with unnecessary bureaucracy, outdated programs or materials, or non-research-based curriculum or instruction. This is evident in the next step of the process.

Once goals for vision attainment have been identified, the next step is to study, in detail, the diversity of academic, developmental, social, and cultural needs of the students. Only then can appropriate choices be made of exactly which curricular materials and instructional strategies will best help reach school, grade-level, or content-area goals. Simply repeating the same things from year to year when society and demographics are changing and then wondering "What is wrong with these kids?" when we know societies and families have changed is "not real smart." We don't have time for "not real smart." We must press onward with forward momentum

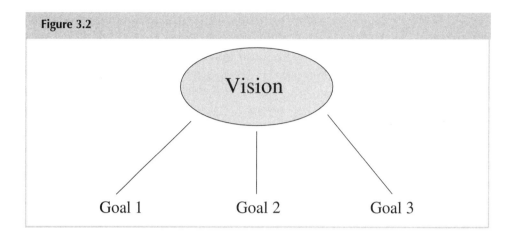

Figure 3.2

Vision

Goal 1   Goal 2   Goal 3

at all times. One definition of insanity is to keep on doing the same things over and over and expecting to get different results. Yet we are doing this in schools all over the United States. We keep trying to teach "the way things used to be" instead of teaching to the students in front of us today. This is late-breaking news, and I don't mean to shock you, so listen up. Beaver Cleaver's class is not coming back. It just isn't. It's gone with the wind, as Scarlet O'Hara would say.

To meet the needs of today's students we must analyze exactly who they are. "What do you mean by that?" you ask. After all, you see the students every day. You know exactly who they are.

But do you really see them? Can teachers in your school immediately tell you or a visitor the specific learning styles, strengths and weaknesses of cognitive development of every student with whom they work without intense study? "That's ridiculous," you say. "No one can do that."

Well, folks, it's time. We don't have time *not* to know everything there is to know about every student. How else can we help every student learn? We cannot continue to keep teaching to the middle segment of the class and hoping all will end well. If we don't know exactly what we are targeting for each student, it is blind luck if we hit it. This is not a smart way to teach. We don't have time for it, our communities deserve better, and the United States is desperately calling out for an improved educational system that addresses the needs of all students, not just the easy to teach. That being the case, we must develop instructional strategies that will meet the individual needs of every student.

To do this, stakeholders must develop, as a team, well-thought-out strategies to reach every goal. As always, when determining goals, the end result should be that nothing that takes place in classrooms is not helping students reach a specific goal that will subsequently help the school attain its vision. When this occurs, we say there is *alignment* between the daily

Figure 3.3

Goal 1:	**Goal 2:**	**Goal 3:**
Strategy 1	Strategy 1	Strategy 1
Strategy 2	Strategy 2	Strategy 2
Strategy 3	Strategy 3	Strategy 3

Figure 3.4

Strategy 1:	**Strategy 2:**	**Strategy 3:**
Resources needed	Resources needed	Resources needed

activities (e.g., curriculum, instruction, programs, etc.) we do each day with a specific goal to help us reach the school vision of excellence.

Let's talk about an example. Say a school's stakeholders have worked to develop a vision of what they want their students and school to be. Next, they continue to study and research to identify specific goals by school, grade, or content area that will help them reach their vision. So let's say stakeholders of a specific school have determined they would like to expand their fine arts department by developing an orchestra program. Their goal would then be to research, develop, procure resources for, and implement an orchestra program. They realize this is a huge goal, one they may not reach in one year. They also know that unless they develop a plan to get the orchestra program going, it will never happen at all. Goals without deadlines are only dreams, so these stakeholders know they must develop an action plan with a time line for implementation and a built-in accountability system to ensure the plan moves forward as scheduled. To do this they identify every single thing that is necessary to get the orchestra program going, including the resources required. They know they must plan for every resource, who will be responsible for what things, and by what deadline (Figure 3.3). In so doing, their action plan becomes aligned with their goals to accomplish their vision of excellence (Figure 3.4).

It is important to understand that to reach targeted goals, necessary resources must be identified and plans for how to get them must be developed. Many resources can be obtained through contributions, volunteers, and other creative endeavors with the community, but there are other things that have to be purchased. Regardless, all resources needed to

Figure 3.5

All Resources ←——————→ Campus Budget

Figure 3.6

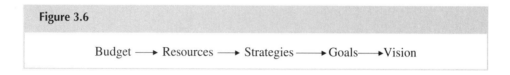

Budget ——→ Resources ——→ Strategies ——→ Goals——→Vision

Figure 3.7

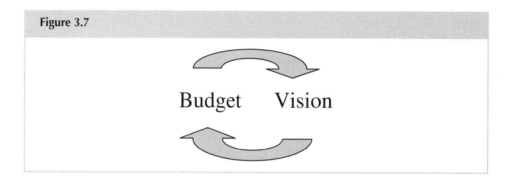

Budget   Vision

accomplish any school goal should be directly connected to the school budget (Figure 3.5). Likewise, everything in the school budget should relate directly to a school goal and need. This is called zero-based budgeting.

Therefore, we should not continue with only slight modifications to a budget from year to year, moving funds around to stay out of the hole but with no true master plan in mind. Creating your budget by aligning it to your vision becomes your master plan for goal attainment (Figure 3.6). In so doing, resources for all school needs and activities are linked to the budget and vice versa (Figure 3.7). Therefore, the school budget is *aligned* with school needs and activities collaboratively developed by teachers, staff, parents, and other members of the school community. This concept of *alignment* is important to all aspects of school leadership. Everything done in schools must be *aligned* with goals and needs.

In summary, for school budget alignment, all resources needed to help the school reach its vision must be budgeted. It is a cyclical process in which the vision drives everything that is done at the school.

The budget is not the only thing that must be aligned with the vision. In like manner, curriculum and instruction must be linked to student, program, and personnel assessment as described in Chapter 4 for Standard 2 (Figure 3.8).

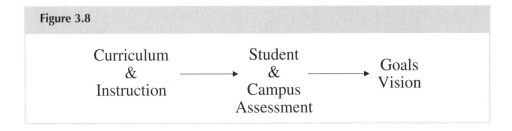

Figure 3.8

Curriculum & Instruction → Student & Campus Assessment → Goals Vision

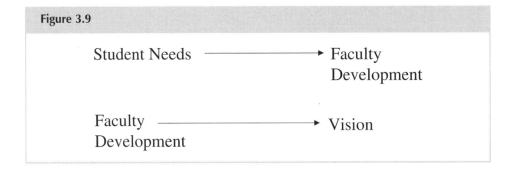

Figure 3.9

Student Needs → Faculty Development

Faculty Development → Vision

Further, staff development also should be based on the factors that faculty and staff have determined could be improved to meet the learning needs of students, rather than what is convenient, easy to arrange, or non-threatening. Because the learning needs of students have all ready been researched, identified, and analyzed as a part of vision and goal development, staff development, also discussed in Chapter 4 for Standard 2, must drive staff development. Thus, staff development must be *aligned* with the school vision and goals as well as the other way around.

The development of a vision and its attainment plan is a time-consuming process if done correctly. This process must not be rushed; allow plenty of time for different concepts to develop and emerge. Anything worth doing is worth doing right, so invest the time necessary to lay this philosophical framework for your school. It is the foundation on which everything else you do is built. If it isn't done right, your foundation will eventually crumble, leaving you and your school in a bad place. Having discussed the collaborative development of a vision and School Improvement Plan in depth, let us now go on to see how to articulate and implement what we have planned.

Articulation of the Vision

Once the school vision, goals, and attainment plan have been collaboratively developed with the input and empowerment of many diverse voices, most people think it is time to put it into place. Doing so at this point is skipping an important step, one that too many people forget. Forgetting this step can set you up for failure, which, of course, we don't want. We want you and your school to be highly successful.

Before putting the plan into place, no matter how wonderful it is, it is critical that there be a separate design for the articulation of the vision, goals, and activities for attainment. Articulation is another word for communication. Before we can implement anything we do in schools, we must let everyone involved know what the plan is, what research and data were used to substantiate the need for it, and how the plan was developed. This is also the time to explain , the plan's purpose, how it will affect—positively and negatively—all school community members, what their roles and responsibilities will be, the implementation time line, and, of course, how the entire process will be assessed. No matter how many people you had involved in the development of the vision, failure to communicate what is going on leaves out a necessary critical mass—the grassroots stakeholders who can either make or break the plan. We don't want our plan sabotaged intentionally or through passive-aggressive behavior. To ensure this won't happen, we will clearly articulate exactly what is happening to anyone who will listen to us. People cannot support what they do not know or understand. Further, people will not support a plan in which they feel they did not have a say. Remember, people support what they help create. It is critical that all aspects of the community be involved in the development, articulation, and the implementation of everything we do. Utilize every means conceivable to do this, whether verbal or written; you might choose to use illustrative stories, including the history, traditions, culture, and legacy of your school.

If there are CAVEs (Citizens Against Virtually Everything) in your community, and we all know there probably are, they should be the first you solicit to be a part of your school planning team. Will they cause you grief up front? Probably. But you never give up on them. Stay professional regardless of what they do. Actively listen to them even when they sound nutty. It is the listening they really care about. They want and need to know that you value their opinion, even when it's crazy. Genuinely and regularly acknowledge their contributions and thoughts. You can do this without saying you agree with a word they say. But you acknowledge them regularly.

The worst thing any leader can do is to make an ordinary person feel ordinary. CAVE people have been disenfranchised along the way from the schools and likely other civic entities as well. To have their intrinsic self-acknowledgement needs met, they create a stink. Your role is to turn their stink into something that smells good. Be patient. Persevere. Mind your manners. Wait for tiny, baby steps forward on their behalf. Praise them for those tiny but important steps. Your goal is to turn these naysayers into the strongest proponents your school has ever had. It won't happen overnight, but it will happen eventually if you stay your course and, as Winston Churchill advised, never, ever, ever give up.

Recently a town changed the parking plan for its downtown area. Immediately afterward, a man was issued a ticket for parking where he should not have. He protested the ticket by saying he did not mind that parking procedures had changed. What he did mind was that they were changed without letting the citizens know what the changes were or when they were going into effect. In essence, what he was complaining about was that there had been no articulation of the plan. This is a trap into which we must be careful not to fall. New administrators in particular fall into this trap. They are so excited to have a great plan developed that they tend to skip the articulation step, thinking it will happen on its own or take care of itself. They go straight to implementing the plan and are surprised when the whole thing eventually comes back to bite them. Don't do that. Algebra teachers advise their students never to skip steps; the same is true here. Together with your team, come up with an articulation design that will provide for the vision, goals, and strategies to be clearly communicated to anyone that will listen. Seek at all times to involve as many people as possible in each step. "Won't that take more time?" you question. Sure, it will. But remember, anything worth doing is worth doing right. So build your firm foundation. Create and implement a strategy to get the word out about the great new vision, enthusiasm, and passion for student-focused success that your school has. Seek to get as many people as possible excited about it, wanting to become involved, and actively engaged in helping teachers teach and students to learn. That, my friends, is articulation of the vision.

Implementation of the Vision

Once the vision has been developed and clearly articulated, it is finally time to implement it. By this point, putting the plan into action becomes easy because every single detail and potential problem has been considered because of the multiple and diverse perspectives that went into its development. So go for it! Have fun! Utilize your leadership skills to motivate those around you to do likewise. Create a school culture and climate of empowerment as you put your plans into effect, encourage innovation and risk taking, and view unsuccessful experiences as simply opportunities to learn. Enjoy putting into effect what we are all about: creating rewarding and supportive learning environments, as well as plans to facilitate student learning and success. This is what our lives as leader educators is all about.

Stewardship of the Vision

People often wonder what exactly "stewardship" of the vision is. One day I want to write an entire book on this topic alone. Like the initial concept of vision, "stewardship" can seem vague, ambiguous, and abstract. So how is a new administrator, working hard to get his or her feet on the ground and the walls to stop spinning, supposed to know or care what this is all about?

That's why you are reading this book. You do care. You want to know. How can you do what is best for your school if you are clueless what this entails? Stewardship of the school vision is part of what makes good eventually become better and then best.

We all know that it is virtually impossible for anyone or any group of people to stay positive, upbeat, cheerful, and optimistic every single day. When this happens to you, it does not mean you have "lost it" or are no longer a good leader or educator. It simply means that you are human. Humans get tired. Humans even make mistakes, although there are those who don't want to admit that. The more tired we get, the more likely we are to make mistakes.

In those instances, you know what? Take a day off. Yes, I said take a day off. I may be the only school board president, ever conscious of tight finances, to tell you that, but listen to me and do it. We spend tons of money each year on conferences and staff development for administrators, counselors, and teachers that really aren't worth a thing. If a single day at home with the covers pulled over your head because you are totally worn out—physically and emotionally—helps you return the next day and be a better person, go for it. Pull those covers right up. Turn off your alarm clock. Just sleep. It is amazing what a decent amount of sleep can do for your body—and your perspective. Earlier we talked in great detail about alignment of various issues. Well, folks, I can guarantee you that there is a direct correlation of fatigue, stress, and anxiety with counterproductivity. Therefore, if you need to stay home and stare mindlessly at the wall all day long, do it. If you need to go outside and dig in the dirt because it satisfies your soul, start digging. How can you be a steward of the vision for others if you are so worn out that you don't remember or care what your school's vision is?

Then, when you return, jump back in the saddle again. It is up to you, as well as the entire school team, to support each other throughout the school year to reach the vision. Your faculty and staff are humans, too.

They have the same physical, psychological, and emotional needs that you have. Organizational research proves no one can leave their personal problems at the workplace door. Our home lives and other aspects of our lives influence everything we do, including what we are doing at work that day. Sometimes our teachers and staff also are at that point of sheer exhaustion that you also reach. At those times, it is up to you to be their mentor and supporter, encouraging them to reflect on what they really need and doing it so they can be the best person and educator that they can be.

As you can see, the results of the things we just described are a gestalt of success, more than the individual strategies by themselves. You are more than being a mentor, supporter, or friend. You are inspiring in them a desire to be more than they are as individuals, to believe in a cause greater than themselves, and to leave a legacy of sustained student success. You are an advocate for all children and the voice of education and social justice in our society. You are the future. What you do to sustain and steward the school vision is important in how you live your life and walk your talk. Talk is cheap and easy. Living up to the high standard of your school vision is hard. Evaluation of the vision must be ongoing, never ending; it must be modified continually for improvement and actively communicated to all stakeholders. Is this an incredibly difficult task? Yes, it is. Are the results worth it? Of course! That's why you're still reading!

Promotion of Community Involvement

If you have been actively soliciting and enticing multiple diverse perspectives and people to participate in the development, articulation, implementation, and stewardship of the school vision, you are well on your way to establishing a solid base of community support. No longer can schools operate in a vacuum. We must be responsive to the growing and difficult needs of the neighborhoods, districts, and societies we serve. Just as no person is an island, neither is any school.

Once the vision is implemented don't just thank all the people who helped you develop it and then let them disappear. Solicit their continued involvement with the school. Never stop working with them to get their ideas of how things are working, how to assess programs and ideas, and how to make things better. Let them know and understand that you truly do care what they think and feel. If they know that, they will walk on water for you and stand beside you firmly when the rough times come. Sooner or later, there's a rough time. You need them as much as the school does. Therefore, you want parents and other community members actively involved in the school. You want to utilize their minds as well as their hands and other resources. The number one question in school leadership—and life—is "How can we make this better?" Whatever the "this" is becomes generic. It can be anything from improving reading comprehension, to lining up students for the buses, to making plans to return to graduate school to pursue or finish an additional certification or degree. The idea is to always and forever be looking for ways you can make everything in your life better, both personally and professionally. Again, anything that makes you a better human being also makes you a better educator. The same goes for everyone else. Solicit, entice, encourage—do whatever it takes to involve and empower as many people as possible from every aspect of the community in the success of your school. For the school to succeed, individual students must succeed. In the end, isn't that what everything we do is supposed to be about?

Now that we have discussed the concept of vision, let's see how it can play itself out in a school setting. Meet Layna Lichenstein, a brand new, scared-to-death principal. See how she deals with issues related to vision. As you read her story, think how you would handle the same situations. After the case study, you will find reflective questions to think about, discuss with others, and react to. Are you ready? Start reading!

PROBLEM-BASED LEARNING

My, Oh, My, What a Mess!

When newcomer Layna Lichenstein was appointed principal of Sybil Watson-Reisner Middle School, she was scared to death. Layna was confident of her abilities, but concerned about her acceptance at a school that had a reputation for being rough and that had never had a female principal before. On arrival, she found a school that was severely divided. Some faculty members barely spoke to each other because of conflict that had arisen over the previous principal being let go. That principal had left with a drinking problem, which he claimed was brought on by job-related stress. Further, another past principal had died of a heart attack. There had been so much staff turnover that few people could remember other principals, but school legend claimed they had had problems as well. Needless to say, Layna had concerns about the school with whose future she had been entrusted, as well as how she would survive the tumultuous waters professionally and personally.

As Layna began talking to faculty, staff, parents, and other community members, it became obvious that this was a school with no vision. Everyone was busy doing his or her own thing as well as trying to take care of other people's business. Layna learned quickly that if they put the same amount of effort into taking care of meeting the needs of their own students, productivity as well as climate would improve considerably. Instead, a culture of negativism had developed and was flourishing.

Because the school had such a poor reputation, expectations for faculty and student performance were low. Not much was expected, and not much was achieved. The students' discipline problems were as much a topic of conversation in the community as the performance of the football team. Layna realized major change efforts were in order. The school was a classic example of an old adage: "If you keep on doing what you have always done, you will keep on getting what you have always gotten." Unfortunately, at Watson-Reisner Middle School, what they were getting wasn't much. Layna thought, "My, oh, my, what a mess! What have I gotten myself into, and what on earth am I going to do about it?"

After countless hours and more than a few sleepless nights, Layna and her Induction Partnership team began to feel better about the future of Watson-Reisner Middle School. Some, although not all, teachers seem genuinely excited that they have a principal who is attempting to exert true leadership and improve the school. They understand that Watson-Reisner has gone steadily downhill over the years because of neglect and lack of fortitude on the part of many people. Other faculty and staff, while not excited, are at least willing to give Layna the benefit of the doubt. Unfortunately, there still are some who think Layna may be just a little bit nuts, has gone overboard, and is trying to make too many changes at the school too quickly. They have taken an attitude of "This too shall pass." After all, it has been forever since any other principal has been with them for more than two years. Why, they wonder, would Layna be any different? If they just wait her out, this principal will be gone too. When she leaves, they reason, so will all her initiatives.

In the meantime, Layna is pleased that at least now the school has a purpose and a plan for success. It may not be the most exhaustive or comprehensive in the world, but at least, for the first time, there is a plan. Many people from the school and the community have worked together to develop it. Now it is time to communicate and market it to the rest of the school, to families, and to the district. She is also well aware that the plan does not yet have everyone's full support. She has heard the rumors and innuendos that she doesn't know what she's doing and is making a bigger mess of an already bad situation. Although she is sensitive to these facts, she is also determined to give Watson-Reisner students every opportunity for success. She has fortitude and is willing to be patient and persistent.

Exercising this patience, Layna soon learns, is a much larger task than she anticipated. Still, she and her Induction Partnership team agree that guaranteeing everyone knows and has consensus about the plan is essential to its implementation and ultimate triumph. They know they must develop a strategy to make sure the plan is put into action in a timely and comprehensive manner while continuing to gather support from additional faculty, staff, students, and families.

REFLECTIVE ANALYSIS

Development of the Vision

1. Layna is self-conscious and insecure about being so overwhelmed by the situation. She is afraid to contact her mentor for fear the perception will be that she is not capable of doing her job. What should she do? Why?

2. Brainstorm various factors that Layna and her mentor should consider as they plan how to address the situation.

3. While appraising the situation, it becomes apparent that the school is not cohesive and has no commonly identified values, joint focus, or goals. Without being didactic or autocratic, develop a process by which Layna and her Induction Partnership team can involve the school community in developing a common vision and core shared values.

Articulation of the Vision

1. With district support and great effort, Layna has gotten multiple stakeholders in the school community to take baby steps toward identifying basic concepts on which they can agree. Design a mechanism by which school and content goals can be identified and strategies for attainment articulated and assessed.

2. In what ways can the process of communicating the vision be accomplished and measured?

Implementation of the Vision

1. What is the distinction between a school vision and school goals? Compare and contrast these concepts. Provide examples.

2. Getting many people involved in the decision-making process is a time-consuming and sometimes frustrating process. It would be much easier simply to announce, "Here are our school vision and

goals. Make them happen." Why is it important to get the buy-in of so many people?

3. Develop and describe a process for implementing the vision. Define roles, responsibilities, and a method for determining accountability.

4. In what ways can data analysis and ongoing assessment be used to implement the vision?

5. Even under the best of circumstances when faculty and the school community do support the vision, there are times of frustration, fatigue, and disgruntlement. Describe strategies you would use to combat "burn out" and other obstacles to ongoing school improvement.

Stewardship of the Vision

1. What does stewardship of the vision mean to you?

2. How can principals promote stewardship of the vision at their schools? In their communities?

3. Design a model by which vision attainment can be assessed, modi-fied, and improved.

4. Maintaining the initial vigor after the initial development, articula-tion, and implementation of the vision has occurred is difficult. In what ways can principals seek to nurture and sustain the steward-ship of the vision?

5. Compare and contrast ways for the Induction Partnership team to nurture and sustain the vision and enthusiasm of the inductee for school leadership.

Promotion of Community Involvement

1. Why is it important for the community to be involved in the develop-ment and nurturance of the school vision? Describe ways to involve the community in the development and support of the vision.

2. How should community involvement in school curricular and cocurricular activities be facilitated?

3. Some parents are hesitant to become involved in school affairs because they lack fluency in English, fear inadequacy, or are inti-midated by the educational system. Brainstorm ways the principal,

faculty, and staff can work together to provide a warm and enticing school climate and culture that would solicit and support parental participation from those with these or similar concerns.

4. On the other hand, there are some parents who come to the school too often. Teachers complain that they cannot teach because they are too busy dealing with parents or coming up with enough for them to do when they visit the classroom. In other words, these parents are in the way. What should the principal do? Elaborate and support your response.

5. Soliciting involvement from parents and the community is often a difficult task, yet these people can offer a valuable and diversified resource of talents, skills, and cultural perspectives. Create a needs assessment by which persons with specific assets can be identified and solicited to enhance student success.

APPLICATION OF THE INDUCTION PARTNERSHIP MODEL

1. Looking at the first six ELCC standards, identify three goals per standard to help Layna develop and grow as an administrator for Sybil Watson-Reisner Middle School.

2. How could the Induction Partnership Model be applied at Watson-Reisner to help her succeed? Elaborate on the basic model to create an individualized growth plan for Layna. Include specific ways she could be assisted to develop, articulate, implement, and provide guidance in the stewardship of a school vision as well as promoting community involvement in this vision.

3. Identify and elaborate on strategies that each of the following stakeholders could offer to help Layna meet her goals for the development, articulation, implementation, and stewardship of the school vision and promoting community involvement with this vision in a collaborative manner:

   - Self
   - Mentor
   - District
   - University or Certifying Agency
   - Business and Community Partnerships
   - Family and Friends

4. What resources will be needed for participants to fulfill their responsibilities? With regard to all stakeholders, how could these resources best be solicited and utilized?

5. Develop accountability measures and a time line for each goal to ensure that growth and assessment are occurring as planned and in a proactive and timely manner.

6. Design an ideal application of the Induction Partnership Model to help you grow in your current situation by creating a culture that values enhanced performance by all stakeholders.

CONCLUSIONS

Throughout this chapter, we have focused on the importance of the development, articulation, implementation, and stewardship of a school vision of learning that promotes maximum knowledge, skills, and dispositions for every student, regardless of his or her situation. We talked about the importance of developing a vision that encompasses everything the school wants to be in the future, rather than settling for what it is today. We learned how to create and align goals, daily activities and strategies, resources, budgets, curriculum, instruction, assessment, and staff development with the vision. We now understand that to work smarter instead of harder, we must align all of these things toward the common purpose of our existence, which is our vision of excellence.

We have talked about the importance of soliciting input and involvement from as many stakeholders as possible from the school community to enhance student performance as well as to empower citizens to take ownership and create pride in the school. I truly cannot stress enough the importance of these factors. Do not consider all of this the "soft stuff" of organizational leadership and management, because these are the things that can make or break your success—and the success of your school. If you or your school do not succeed, it is worse than a shame. It's just not right. We want you to be successful and for your school to be even more successful. John Maxwell (1995) says you can't build a reputation on what you are going to do. You build your reputation on what you have done. As new principals, it is essential that you develop specific and targeted plans to enhance your skills in working with and motivating those around you. If you fail to plan, you are planning to fail. Begin now to plan how you can use the Induction Partnership Model to maximize your success as well as that of those around you.

ACTIVITIES FOR ADMINISTRATOR INDUCTION AND PROFESSIONAL DEVELOPMENT

The Standards-Based "Sweet 16" Induction Developmental Activities

- Hold an off-campus retreat before the school year begins to facilitate team building, development of the vision, and the creation of activities to support it.
- Include administration, staff, and local community representatives in the initial and ongoing development, articulation, implementation, and assessment of the school vision.
- As a team, develop a vision articulation plan for the larger community that will ensure success for all students.
- Develop a program in which community stakeholders have numerous opportunities to serve the school in a variety of ways.
- Develop activities and functions that involve the school community so they will share and support the vision.
- As a school, work on interpersonal and communication skills to be able to gain support from the school community for the school vision, goals, and activities.
- Provide staff development to enhance the teaching and learning that are necessary to accomplish the school vision.
- Ensure the school vision is posted in every classroom and other strategic areas where staff, students, parents, and visitors can easily see and be reminded of it.
- As a team of teachers, administrators, parents, and other members of the community, discuss school needs and brainstorm ways to achieve them.
- Visit successful schools to observe how they articulate and create synergy for their vision as well as how they implement these strategies successfully within their school communities.
- Invite administrators and teachers from highly successful schools with demographics similar to yours to visit your school. Discuss strategies they have used that have been successful, how to provide stewardship for the vision, and how to avoid staff burnout.
- Provide faculty training and support to assess effectiveness of school activities that support each goal.
- Encourage teachers and staff throughout the year with praise and mementos based on an original, schoolwide theme chosen at the beginning of the year.

- Analyze current school programs to discern if they are serving the vision appropriately. Continue, modify, adjust, or eliminate them as needed.
- Collect, interpret, and analyze multiple sources of data for ongoing school modifications and improvement.
- Have regular meetings to assess where the school is, evaluate progress, modify plans, and celebrate accomplishments.

4 The Best We Can Be

If you have always done it that way, it is probably wrong.

—Charles Kettering

STANDARD 2

Candidates who complete the program are educational leaders who have the knowledge and ability to promote the success of all students by promoting a positive school culture, providing an effective instructional program, applying best practice to student learning, and designing comprehensive professional growth plans for staff.

TOP TEN THINGS ADMINISTRATORS WISH THEY HAD KNOWN BEFORE ENTERING THE PRINCIPALSHIP

Principals must

1. Be instructional leaders as well as operational managers.

2. Have knowledge of appropriate instructional techniques including brain-based research, learning styles, coaching strategies, and other strategies designed for student developmental interests and needs.

3. Facilitate quality instruction and provide guidance for faculty development based on identified school and student needs.

4. Have a complete understanding of all school programs.

5. Be thoroughly knowledgeable about special education laws and procedures, including the referral process; admission, review, and dismissal meetings; Individuals with Disabilities Education Act (IDEA), and so forth.

6. Know and be able to apply the similarities and differences of the discipline process for general and special education students.

7. Know, understand, and implement policies and procedures in regard to at-risk student populations as determined by federal, state, and local standards.

8. Read the policy manual or ask someone if they don't know something. A principal must never guess.

9. Have specific job descriptions with detailed responsibilities and evaluative processes for all positions.

10. Analyze the history and current status of school performance for all students on standardized tests and state exams, including strengths, weaknesses, and demographic subgroups, to facilitate and improve effective instructional programs and best practice.

PHILOSOPHICAL FRAMEWORK

California's Silicon Valley is known throughout the world as the epitome of technological innovation. Because of the creative thinking and risk taking of untold numbers of people, ideas generated there have literally changed the world through the way we communicate, work with, and manage data. There is a perception that bright people sit around all day in Silicon Valley dreaming up wonderful new things to make our lives better.

To a certain extent this is true. What the average citizen does not realize, however, is that most of the new ideas that come from Silicon Valley are complete failures and utterly useless. They never amount to anything. But the good ideas they do come up with have revolutionized technology. We experience the benefits of these innovations every single day in ways of which we are not even aware.

"How," you might ask, "can they continue to develop such wonderful ideas if most of them don't work?" You'd think the frustration of multiple unsuccessful ventures would stifle creativity, yet that hasn't happened. Why?

It's because in Silicon Valley they have established a culture of high expectations, risk taking, and continuous improvement of their own best practices; this sparks and drives their talents. It is their standard expectation never to settle for the way things have been done in the past. They never rest on past accomplishments. Yesterday's accomplishments are a thing of the past. Silicon Valley innovators are continuously pushing forward, always competing to be the best in the world at what they do.

That, my friends, is establishing and sustaining an organizational culture that thrives on stimulus and change, continuous assessment, and best practices; this, in turn, perpetuates creativity and growth. If employees in the cutthroat world of Silicon Valley can change the technological world by using these skills, there is no reason we as school leaders should not be doing the same thing. Saying these things and accomplishing them are far different matters, however. Having the passion for this innovative vision is terrific, but it is only a start toward maximizing organizational productivity. Getting others to buy into and commit to it is much more difficult.

Brand new principals are often fired up with idealism, or at least we hope they are. Then they hit another example of the cold, dark world we call reality. They learn that leading and managing a school is different from what they understood through textbooks, internships, and prior experience. Too soon, they encounter the teacher's-lounge lizards who are there simply to draw a paycheck, not to make a significant difference in the lives of students and families. They meet the resident control freaks and reencounter the CAVE people, those "Citizens Against Virtually Everything" we met in Chapter 3. I hope there are also good folks around as well who are always ready to help sustain the stewardship of the vision. Still, it is particularly difficult for new principals to come in and create lasting change without getting run off the property in the process.

Promote Positive School Culture

Here we go again with another of those abstract terms. We know what culture is in relation to race or heritage, but what do we mean by the culture of a school? How can a school have culture? According to our friend *Webster's New World College Dictionary* (Agnes, 2001), culture is "the ideas, customs, skills, arts, etc. of a people or group that are transferred, communicated, or passed along as in or to succeeding generations; Such ideas, customs, etc. of a particular people or group in a particular period or civilization; The particular people or group having such ideas, customs, etc." To apply this definition to schools, a school culture then would be the ideas, customs, skills, arts, and so forth of the faculty, staff, students, principal, and other stakeholders that make it unique and different from other schools. If a school climate is the way it feels at a certain school, the culture would be the way the school does things. Both the culture and climate of every school will be different just as all schools are different.

So what is the big deal about a school culture? It's a big deal because you as principal set the stage for the climate and way we do things on that individual school. If the principal has a status quo attitude, has no vision, is schooled in management but not leadership, and does not have high expectations to ensure high standards and expectations of performance by every member of the learning team, not much is going to happen, and virtually nothing is going to change or improve. Why should it? Of whom little is expected, little is received.

On the other hand, if the principal values high-performance expectations from everyone in the school—including students, teachers, staff, parents, and so on—then more will be achieved. It is that basic philosophy of "you reap what you sow." You reap what you expect. If you don't expect much, you won't get much. If you expect a lot, you will get a lot. But as long as you keep on doing what you've always done, you will keep on getting the same results you have always received. For new or experienced principals, this is a basic premise on which every other facet of school leadership is built. You must be forward thinking and a risk taker; you must always aim for the top, both professionally and personally.

Some beginning and experienced principals have difficulty understanding and applying this standard because they say they are not the "rah-rah" cheerleader type of school leaders. They feel that they can never reach this standard because of their innate personality style. It is important for their Induction Partnership team and others to clarify for them that a "rah-rah" attitude is helpful but not required to provide leadership and to ensure a positive school culture. You can be a low-key leader and still be an effective one. Factors more important than your personality type are your dedication, commitment, and ability to articulate the school vision, culture, and climate to guarantee that every student has an equal opportunity to learn to the best of their ability and beyond.

It is not enough to say, "OK, Y'all, this year we are going to be real positive around here. We're going to expect the best out of everyone, you hear? And that does include you!" The school community is likely to respond, "Yeah, right, Buster. Just who do you think you are? Sit back and watch, because we're going to show you just exactly what we will or will not do!" So although you lead the change process for enhancement of a positive school culture, you cannot dictate it. You can only mold it by letting your walk match your talk and by being an administrator who leads through example. The entire philosophy and all relevant concepts must be discussed collaboratively and at great length to determine whether the school community really buys into it, for what reasons, and why or why not. If so, how can a plan for creating or enhancing a positive school culture be developed, articulated, implemented, and continually assessed to ascertain if progress is being made toward this goal? If progress is not occurring, what modifications must be made to see to it that it does happen in a timely manner?

This positive school culture and climate is also not limited to the dominant student population within the school. The school comprises students from diverse populations and of both genders; students may speak different languages, have disabilities; they come from various races and socioeconomic groups. Students in each of these groups must be honored and respected as integral parts of the school. Each facet of students' heritage and personalities must be valued and used to enhance the total school culture. Remember that simply acknowledging the presence of diverse populations is not enough. We must appreciate their presence and utilize their talents to make us a stronger, more unified whole. In so doing, we create a family or team atmosphere in school such that everyone feels they are "in this together." We are not competitive, but supportive and nurturing to help each other succeed, just the way we should be within our families. In this manner, our school community becomes and behaves as an extended family network for the benefit of all students and the community.

Provide Effective Instructional Programs

Since the appearance of Ron Edmonds's (1979, 1983) effective school research, we have heard much about the principal being the instructional leader of the school. Some new principals are terrified at the prospect of needing to be the expert on all curriculum and instruction taught at their schools, particularly on content areas that they feel they have not mastered. Yet even though you are the instructional leader, there is nothing that requires you to be the expert in all forms of language, mathematics, science, technology, history, and civic responsibility. What you are required to do is to understand and facilitate appropriate processes for curriculum enhancement and developmentally appropriate instructional methods. Your goal is to know and be able to facilitate actions that apply theories of effective instruction to advance the level and application of diversified curriculum resources and advanced instructional strategies. You are the facilitator of these areas, not the sole provider of them. There is a difference. Be careful to notice the distinction between being able to facilitate the successful progress of teachers and others, rather than doing everything yourself. If you try to do that, you will kill yourself. Once dead, there isn't anything you can do to help anyone, so budget your time.

Enhance, empower, and develop others to facilitate success. You cannot do everything alone. Remember that. Work with your Induction Partnership team to create a support plan as you seek ways to seek resources, select appropriate teacher leaders, and empower others to enhance teaching and learning. Together, let them guide you in ways that have worked for them, to learn how to study the appropriate data, to be able to provide school leadership in recommending—not requiring—the development, implementation, and assessment of curricular programs and instructional strategies that are appropriate for the different needs of individual students.

Will faculty sometimes balk at the idea of individualizing to meet targeted student needs? Probably. They are rightly concerned about the time it will take to research and analyze exactly what those needs are. But without doing this, we are teaching to the middle of the class and not meeting the needs of those on the perimeters. It is doubtful that any of you will develop a school vision that says you will only teach to the middle portion of the population while hoping the best for those at either end of the bell curve. To make your vision real, there must be specific plans for meeting the needs of every learner, including those who are severely disabled, come from other cultures, or have different learning and living styles, as well as those who have goals in medicine, law, engineering, accounting, technology, the arts, or wherever their dreams lie. Each student deserves an equitable opportunity to make his or her dreams come true. Besides, our vision requires it. If it doesn't, it is time to change it. For those who just can't make themselves buy into the all-encompassing passion of the diversity of the vision, I just have one piece of advice. Get a different job.

Assessment of forward and consistent movement toward the attainment of effective instructional programs must be ongoing. Ongoing means all the time. It does not mean just at the end of the year when reports are due. It means that every day you must be asking, "How can we make this better?" and you must ask this about everything that is done in your school. Further, you should be instilling this same reflective questioning in all members of the school community. Nothing should be immune. Programs that have been there forever, but are no longer beneficial or cost effective should either be modified or eliminated. Everything conceivable should be assessed for appropriate enhancement of teaching and learning. Technological tools and information systems can be used for both quantitative and qualitative evaluation and research measures. When weak spots or unwanted trends are identified, it is your responsibility to guide and provide assistance for improvement. Remember, it is not your job to do everything yourself, but to be able to facilitate the development of an improvement plan, to articulate and implement that plan, and to assess it continually for improvement. As a school leader, then, you are always on red alert for potential school improvements that will help teachers do their jobs effectively and help all students learn to their maximum potential and reach their dreams.

Apply Best Practices to Student Learning

Good teaching doesn't happen through luck or chance. It must be continuously refined to meet the changing needs of today's students. What worked last year or even last month may not work now. Today's students are much more diverse than those from the past. They come to school with different issues on their minds that distract from their learning processes and, worse, from their desire to learn. As principal you are responsible for addressing the teachers who keep wishing things could "go back the way they used to be." Some teachers do this overtly, and others gripe about it silently. Still, the resistance to change is present and often too clearly evident. This is what we do not want.

What we do want is for all faculty, staff, and other members of the school community not only to understand that Beaver Cleaver's class is not coming back, not only to accept this, but to embrace the changing ethnicity of classrooms of today and tomorrow. We are not going back in time. We are going forward. Students who were totally disenfranchised from the educational process a generation ago are present in schools today. The questions become these: What are we doing to do about it? How are we going to address their learning needs? What can we do to help them?

The application of best instructional practices is a key to enhancing student performance. Why reinvent the wheel when it has all ready been invented? Work smarter, not harder. With some exceptions, most teachers are working hard and do want to help each student learn. They are already doing all they know to do. They are not deliberately ignoring better methods. They just don't know they exist.

That's where you and your Induction Partnership team come in. You may or may not have a clue about how to find ways to improve curriculum and instruction on your school. Together with your team, however, you can find ways to explain to your faculty and staff the methods to find and use suitable research tools that will enhance a learning culture and climate for superior and diversified student accomplishments.

Your role is to ensure that being the instructional leader is not just a title, but a meaningful representation of who you are, what you stand for, and how you accomplish the appropriate and best instructional practices for your school. How do you apply adult learning theories to help the teachers learn established best practices used in other places? How can you assist them in researching, finding, analyzing, and applying best practices for the unique needs of your students? How do you motivate them to have an ongoing, sincere concern for diversity in student learning processes? All of these things are important and relevant issues to discuss with your Induction Partnership team to gain informative feedback. You may not know what to do, but together as a team, you can utilize one another's perspectives and connections to create synergy for teacher empowerment in the process for enhanced student performance. The time required to do this successfully will vary from person to person and situation to situation. Both quality and quantity of time invested are important issues. Remember, what you will get out of this will be in direct proportion to the amount of effort you put into it. To grow, we must stretch ourselves. Stretching out of our comfort zones is uncomfortable and can generate resistance from various stakeholders. That's why each member of the team must be invested in the ongoing success of the process.

Design Comprehensive Professional Growth Plans

When I was a little girl my parents had a weekend home in a quiet country place called Indian Lake. I liked being able to walk around all by myself and felt perfectly safe in the outdoors—except for the rattlesnakes, which I vigilantly avoided.

Not too far from our house but separate from the lake was a small pond. Different from the lake that had a steady, slow influx of water from the nearby Sabine River, this pond just sat there. It sometimes had lily pads and turtles might emerge to sun, which I liked, but otherwise the pond had lots of algae and really wasn't very pretty. The reason for the algae was that the lake had become stagnant. There was no new influx of water, so the pond just sat there turning green.

The same is true in our schools. When we do not have a clearly defined and articulated vision of excellence, the ideas that are already present in the school just sit there. It's a classic example of "If you keep on doing what you've always done, you'll keep on getting what you have always gotten." Researching, analyzing, and applying new learning theories and best research-based practices are important. Without them, there is no fresh water. The school becomes stagnant. Who wants a stagnant school? Not us! So we press on with our school goals and strategies that will lead us one step at a time toward our vision of excellence. As discussed in Chapter 3, we make sure our curriculum, instruction, assessment, resources, budgets, and staff development are aligned with our school vision.

The same is true for our teachers, staffs, and ourselves—we, too, do not want to become stagnant. John Hoyle (2002) of Texas A&M University says a lot of people like to give lip service to embracing change, but, in truth, the only people who actually like change are wet babies. For everyone else, change pushes us out of our comfort zones and makes us feel nervous and somewhat insecure. When push comes to shove, this is what makes any kind of a change process difficult to implement and sustain. In truth, people don't like it. They like things just the way they are, even if that isn't what is best for their students.

It is our role as school leaders to change that paradigm. We've discussed doing that for the school itself through the development of the vision and school improvement and goal attainment plans. But what about personnel improvement, particularly for teachers who have been teaching in a certain manner for at least a thousand years and truly see no reason to change? They want the students to change, not themselves. Well, we know the students are indeed changing, but not likely in the way these teachers would prefer.

In business and industry they use the term "retooling" to address this issue. As methods and techniques have been successful in the past become outdated or fail to maximize organizational productivity, new ones must be learned. These new skills are part of the "retooling" process.

We must do the same thing. We must "retool" personally and professionally to keep from falling into a rut so deep we can never change. As a beginning administrator, it's the perfect time for you to implement this process because some change is always inevitable with a new leader. The trick is how to introduce the idea of individual professional development plans without appearing haughty, condescending, or downright arrogant. "Who is this new weirdo who thinks she can come in here and tell us what to do? We were here before she arrived and we will be here after she's gone!"

The best way to do that is to lead by example, by being honest and upfront. This is also a perfect tool to use with your Induction Partnership team, which is all about helping you grow personally and professionally. People can always sense a fraud, but they also always respond to people who are genuine and authentic. Why not tell them the truth?

Tell them that you are working with an Induction Partnership Team to help you grow and develop as an administrator as well as a human being. Tell them who is on your team, what their roles and responsibilities are, and an overview of the things you plan to address first. You don't have to tell them your life history, but do tell them enough to let them know you are talking to them from your heart, about your own growth, that you are sincere, and that from time to time you will be soliciting their formative input to help you succeed. Who could argue with that?

In so doing, you are also setting the stage to ask them to do likewise. In the same manner that you collaboratively developed the vision and the goals and strategies for its attainment, faculty and staff can be assisted to develop their own vision of who they want to be, their goals to help them get there, and the things they must do to make that happen. By having shared with them the process you are using, they can see that you are not just spouting rhetoric to them. You truly do value the importance of planning for lifelong learning in your own life. Your walk is matching your talk. This breeds trust and credibility. Those are two things that money cannot buy but that are essential to your success as an administrator and as a person.

Your role is to help them succeed. When teachers are happy and successful, their students will be as well. There is a big overlap between the personal lives and school lives among both teachers and students. You simply cannot leave your private life at the schoolhouse door, no matter how hard you try. It is part of who you are. Stress that you value being a lifelong learner to the point that you have put together a team of people to help you create your own goals and things to do that reach them. You are setting time lines for each step in the process to make sure that your own growth isn't getting pushed to the back burner, till things settle down, or, in truth, will never happen. Things never will settle down. That's the nature of school leadership. There is always something big going on.

Once they see your walk matching your talk you will have credibility. You will not be a leader who says one thing but does another. You will not set a certain standard of behavior for others but think you are immune (a habit discussed in Chapter 7). You therefore can plan staff development that is purpose driven, that will help faculty reach their own personal goals as well as those that address identified school areas of concern. Your role is one of a shepherd. You are there to care for and nurture your flock, not to do everything for them.

The staff development your school provides should be collaboratively created, based on faculty input and school needs, so that it is context specific for your school at a given moment in time. Again, research and analytical skills are important as people work together to identify exactly what the needs are; what the development program should look like; who should deliver it, how and when; and how it will be assessed. Methods such as classroom observations, discussions, collaborative reflection, and adult-learning strategies should be used to help develop these plans. What is appropriate staff development this year may or may not be appropriate again next year because students, teachers, staff, and school needs will change. This means you get to repeat this process every single year. Until you retire, you will be the shepherd of your school. Take care of your flock! Remember, when they grow and succeed, the students do as well. When all of them are successful, so are you. That's what this is all about.

PROBLEM-BASED LEARNING

There's Got to Be a Morning After

Frio Canyon Middle School was long recognized as a high-performing school. It was designated as a state mentor school to assist other schools as they sought to develop a teaming approach to enhance the learning performance of young adolescents. After the retirement of the principal, who had been there many years, district administrator Bryant Riley was appointed to the job. There was immediate excitement within the school community because Bryant's reputation for being student centered as well as his focus on high expectations and making learning creative and fun were well known. Bryant began the job energized and looking forward to the new challenge before him.

Before the school year began, Bryant called the faculty and staff together to discuss the future vision for Frio Canyon. The faculty took the opportunity seriously to reflect and reexamine where they had been, what they had accomplished, where they wanted to go, and what they wanted their school to become. Together they decided that their past accomplishments were just that—in the past. Collectively they agreed it was time to redefine their vision, set new goals, and step out of their comfort zone of the "way we have been doing things" at Frio Canyon. They realized this entailed far more than a single day's work. First, they recognized that they must analyze and synthesize various current and cumulative student data. They knew they must also ascertain school as well as student individual learning strengths and weaknesses. They must then spend significant amounts of time researching best practices to improve their instructional programs so they could optimally meet the needs of Frio Canyon students and their families. A plan was eventually developed and roles identified to allow everyone to become empowered in the process. Input was sought from parents and other community members, considered equal partners on the learning team.

As time went by at Frio Canyon, Bryant and the team discovered an increasing trend in the number of English as a second language (ESL) students attending the school. Although this had been gradually occurring over a period of time, no specific initiatives had been developed to identify and meet the needs of these learners beyond the hiring of an ESL teacher.

Classroom instructors felt unprepared to target these unique students needs and thus had received specialized attention only in the ESL classroom. They had otherwise been absorbed into regular classes with no specialized instructional strategies.

This pattern had received vastly varying results. Although some of the ESL learners appeared to be making the transition to English with ease, many others were not. Disaggregated test scores showed a significant difference in the learning performance of ESL versus students whose primary language was English. Bryant and the teachers realized with dismay that although they thought they previously had met the needs of all their students, they no longer were. Many of the teachers who had been at Frio Canyon a long time were sincerely grieved at the findings and immediately wanted to know what they could do to rectify the situation.

After researching best practices, Bryant, the faculty and staff, as well as members of the community, sought additional input from other schools that had also experienced similar changing demographics. They made school visits, created Internet discussion groups, and sought expert advice as a team. They targeted families of ESL learners and made home and neighborhood visits to gain parental and community perspectives. Although no one ever made a home visit alone, to facilitate fluent communication they often were able to take someone with them who spoke the primary home language. Parents of all students were invited to the school for a series of bilingual "School Conversations" during which needs and future directions for the school were openly discussed. Child care was provided. The purpose of the meetings was to determine how Frio Canyon could work together with the community to develop a program that would maximize student learning through research, best practice, and cultural contexts for their school.

By the end of December, a model had been developed collaboratively that most of the faculty, staff, and families were excited about. Staff development was planned to help all persons dealing with students to enhance their ESL skills. Various community members made commitments for different roles to assist students on a regular basis. All in all, nearly everyone was looking forward to the changes that would take place at Frio Canyon after the holidays. Bryant thought, "Hey, this changing of a school's culture is a piece of cake! Things are going great here!"

When you least expect it, disaster falls. When school reopened after the winter break, the new strategies were implemented as projected. As time went by, however, fatigue and stress set in because of mandatory statewide standardized testing to meet the federal requirements of "No Child Left Behind" legislation. The closer time came to testing, the higher faculty anxieties rose. The combination of implementing new strategies with a diversified population combined with the stress of high-stakes testing began to take its toll. Frustration built as teachers started quibbling with students and each other. As everyone knows, preadolescents are unique unto themselves even under the best of circumstances. The combination of puberty, student and faculty stress over the new testing program, and nerves being on edge created a situation that was volatile at best. Every day brought more disruptions—students getting into fights; rumors or evidence of drugs, alcohol, or gang activity; teachers getting on their own and each others' nerves. It seemed like a new student was turning up pregnant all the time. Upset parents began calling or coming by to discuss things that, under normal circumstances, would not have been issues. The snowball effect of a school losing control was in place.

Bryant began to worry that his superintendent would hear about the problems and expect answers. Before he knew it, teachers were complaining that he brought in too much change all at once and that he didn't know what he was doing instructionally; they said they wanted to go back to the way things used to be with their former principal, the Living Legend. Few stopped to consider that the demographics at Frio Canyon had changed, regardless of who was in charge. In addition, the testing and accountability system required by "No Child Left Behind" was not something over which Bryant, their district, or anyone else had control. Although Bryant tried to stay upbeat and positive, internally, he was completely worn out. He thought, "How can I make this better? How can I defuse this situation? How on earth did this happen when things were going so well? Where is someone to help me rekindle my own stewardship of the vision so I can help the school rekindle its own? Somebody help me, please!"

REFLECTIVE ANALYSIS

Promote Positive School Culture

1. Bryant is particularly concerned about the disintegration of the positive school culture and climate that existed at Frio Valley during his early months. How can the Induction Partnership Model be used to regain and promote a positive culture on school?

2. Out of concern for his job, Bryant did not keep his superintendent informed of school problems and the declining climate as the spring semester progressed. Was this a good idea? Why or why not?

3. With a partner, role-play potential, uncomfortable discussions with a superintendent or other supervisor. Develop possible best

approaches for Bryant to inform and solicit advice from this person while also avoiding disaster and anxiety.

4. Identify substantive ideas to help new principals develop relationships with their supervisors that are based on mutual trust and respect.

5. In what ways can you empower your current school to improve the school culture and climate to maximize teaching and learning?

Provide Effective Instructional Programs

1. How can Bryant help the faculty members regain clarity about meeting student needs when they are so stressed?

2. What are the first things Bryant should do to improve instructional strategies?

3. In what ways should faculty be involved in evaluation and decision making regarding plans already implemented?

Apply Best Practices to Student Learning

1. Devise an assessment plan to address best practice of instructional techniques in place at your school.

2. Should parents and other community members be involved in the process of instructional assessment? Why or why not? If so, in what ways?

Design Comprehensive Professional Growth Plans

1. Bryant realized the staff development that had been planned and implemented before the end of December had not been adequate to prepare teachers for the complexity of what they were undertaking. Describe a process by which Bryant could directly involve and empower teachers in assisting to plan their own professional growth.

2. Bryant also failed to consider the added impact of the new high-stakes testing program on faculty and student morale and stress levels. What would a more proactive approach have been?

3. Under the circumstances, what can be done about it now?

4. Bryant firmly believes that all members of the school community should establish both personal and professional mission statements with identified goals and strategies toward their attainment. He believes that when each person has a sense of direction in their lives, it helps them identify personal and professional identity, thus providing focus for their lives. Is the development of a personal mission statement appropriate as a staff developmental activity if it is a private activity? Why or why not?

5. From an individual growth perspective, in what ways can you facilitate members of your school community to identify personal and professional goals and their attainment?

APPLICATION OF THE INDUCTION PARTNERSHIP MODEL

1. Looking at the first six ELCC standards, identify three goals per standard to help Bryant develop and grow as an administrator for Frio Canyon Middle School.

2. How could the Induction Partnership Model be applied at Frio Canyon to help Bryant succeed? Elaborate on the basic model to create an individualized growth plan for Bryant. Include specific ways he could be assisted to develop in the areas of providing effective instructional programs, applying best practice to student learning, and designing comprehensive professional growth plans for faculty and staff in a collaborative manner.

3. Identify and elaborate on strategies for each of the following that stakeholders could implement to help Bryant meet his goals for providing effective instructional programs, applying best practice to student learning, and designing comprehensive professional growth plans for faculty and staff in a collaborative manner.
   • Self
   • Mentor
   • District
   • University or Certifying Agency
   • Business–School Community Partnerships
   • Family and Friends

4. What resources will be needed for each participant to fulfill his or her responsibilities? Utilizing all stakeholders, how could these resources best be solicited and utilized?

5. Develop accountability measures and a time line for each goal to ensure growth and assessment are occurring as planned and in a proactive and timely manner. Determine as a team how these issues can be brought before the group on a continuing basis to ensure development is taking place.

6. Design an ideal application of the Induction Partnership Model to help you grow in your current situation in regard to creating a culture that values enhanced performance by all stakeholders.

CONCLUSIONS

In this chapter, I have discussed the importance of creating and nurturing a strong school culture and climate that is conducive to student, faculty, staff, and personal development. I have discussed the development, utilization, and assessment of an effective instructional program as well as the need to research, analyze, and apply best practices for the success of all students. Finally, I discussed how important having and utilizing a personal and professional staff development plan is for both you and your staff to ensure lifelong learning. Each of these elements is a spoke that holds up your school vision umbrella on those rainy days that always seem to show up when you least need them. Together with your Induction Partnership team they are the strong framework you can depend on to carry you through when times are tough. They won't let you down, but they can't help you if you don't use them. The choice is yours.

ACTIVITIES FOR ADMINISTRATOR INDUCTION AND PROFESSIONAL DEVELOPMENT

The Standards-Based "Sweet 16" Induction Developmental Activities

- Create and consistently expect a culture of high expectations from all stakeholders.
- Be positive, visible, and enthusiastic to foster a nurturing and supportive learning environment.
- Develop and implement strategies to recognize schoolwide academic achievement.
- Take staff and faculty members on field trips to observe other schools to facilitate answers to questions and get new ideas to enhance innovative practice and student learning.

- Provide mentors to assist with the questions and problems of new teachers. Sustain this through bimonthly induction meetings to address curriculum, instruction, and classroom management issues.
- Develop a mentor program for at-risk students that incorporates community input, resources, and support.
- Have the faculty complete a needs assessment to identify and address school concerns. Follow up to ensure that progress is being made and needs are being met.
- Facilitate the brainstorming of ideas to enhance school culture, traditions, heritages, and celebrations.
- Research common elements of school climate and culture found in successful schools and analyze whether they could be adapted to enhance yours.
- Organize faculty and staff appreciation luncheons to show regular support for their hard work.
- Facilitate cross-grade and cross-subject team meetings to enhance student learning through curricular integration as well as vertical and horizontal alignment.
- Analyze school data to identify student needs. Brainstorm and discuss with the school community new ideas that could be implemented to address them.
- Through questionnaires, surveys, and interviews, solicit insights from parents and staff on the school learning environment and how to maximize student productivity.
- Develop strategies to become more comfortable communicating with parents and other community members.
- Develop a committee to facilitate celebrating different cultures within the school community.
- Provide times and areas for the school community to display and discuss personal items that instill a better understanding and appreciation for diverse cultures and traditions.
- Meet with individual teachers to individualize professional goals and provide developmental support for their needs.

5 How Do I Run This Place?

It takes less time to do a thing right, than it does to explain why you did it wrong.

—Henry Wadsworth Longfellow

STANDARD 3

Candidates who complete the program are educational leaders who have the knowledge and ability to promote the success of all students by managing the organization, operations, and resources in a way that promotes a safe, efficient, and effective learning environment.

TOP TEN THINGS ADMINISTRATORS WISH THEY HAD KNOWN BEFORE ENTERING THE PRINCIPALSHIP

Principals must

1. Be organized!
   - Document everything (parent, student, teacher, and community member conferences, phone calls, etc.).
   - Know the correct contact person and telephone number for anything that could arise.

- Understand the importance of establishing and keeping routines with consistency.
- Create and stay on top of committees that are beneficial to the school and helpful to you. If they are not, get rid of them. They are a waste of time.

2. Understand and budget time.
   - Ensure there is enough time provided for schoolwide projects.
   - Allow more time than you think needed for resolving student, teacher, parent, and community problems, conflicts, and crises.
   - Get to know students by walking the halls, visiting lunch periods, talking with them individually and in groups.
   - Spend the majority of the day out of the office.
   - Take care of people during the day and paperwork later.

3. Understand and facilitate the role and responsibilities of school support staff including assistant principals, counselors, secretaries, paraprofessionals, custodians, and others. They are powerful.

4. Understand the school's special programs to provide effective leadership and management.

5. Create a system to know the location of all school resources (e.g., equipment, furniture, supplies, test data, student records, etc.) at all times.

6. Lead, model, and motivate teachers for better classroom management, fact finding, decision making, and instruction.

7. Facilitate school success by cultivating positive relationships with the maintenance, custodial, and other support staff.

8. Always be visible and available.

9. Know the character of the people surrounding you. It will show during a crisis.

10. Actively listen to learn the other person's perspective in conflict resolution and decision making.

PHILOSOPHICAL FRAMEWORK

On February 1, 2003, my husband and I were relaxing and enjoying a wonderful, quiet weekend with friends at a small, enchanting lodge near Palestine, Texas, called Crystal Lake. There are no televisions, radios, fax machines, or Internet connections at Crystal Lake. In fact, our cellular telephones wouldn't even connect to service. In other words, it is a place for complete quiet and rest for your soul. We were contentedly nestled in with a huge fireplace behind the East Texas Pine Cone Curtain.

Then the space shuttle *Columbia* blew up literally over our heads. The windows shook and the men wondered aloud what on earth was taking place. We women, of course, slept through the whole thing. It wasn't until later in the morning that we heard what had happened. We grieved with the rest of America at the tragic loss of seven valiant and brave astronauts including the very first from Israel. As you have heard, there was debris all over that part of Texas, particularly where we were because *Columbia* blew up on top of us. We were able to see pieces up close but weren't allowed to touch them because of concerns of toxicity or radioactivity. Still, it was a gruesome and somber time as we stood together with close friends and experienced how short life is and how suddenly things can tragically change.

At the time of this writing, NASA is still trying to determine exactly what went wrong. There are many thoughts on the subject by those inside and outside of NASA, but no definitive answers. More data analysis is needed, as well as study of the debris itself and its projections as it hit earth. The truth is, we just don't know yet what went wrong. As my precious mother used to say, "The devil is in the details." NASA is searching hard for the details to find those answers.

The same thing is true in school leadership. We can talk all day about the vision and culture of the school, but as David Erlandson of Texas A&M University is fond of saying, "It's hard to keep your eyes on the mission of the school when the walls are falling down." When Dr. Mike Moses accepted the position of general superintendent of the Dallas Independent School District (ISD), the district had multiple problems. One of the largest urban districts in the country, Dallas school board meetings had become such debacles that many citizens were embarrassed. Student achievement was not where it needed to be across all demographics, and many buildings were in need of significant structural repair. Some walls really *were* falling down. The district was such a mess that some people were saying it was just too large and unwieldy to be productive. Various ideas were passed around, including everything from sending in a state monitor to dividing the district into various smaller ones.

Then Mike Moses came in as superintendent. Mike is an old friend of mine, so people repeatedly asked me why I thought he would take such a seemingly impossible job. I said to them, "Mike is a person who thrives on a challenge." He's just like me! Furthermore, if anyone could pull Dallas ISD back together, Mike could. If he couldn't, well, it just couldn't be done.

Just as I predicted, he has done it. From the beginning, Mike has worked with the city and the citizens themselves to take care of the business of running a huge school district. A needs assessment showed that multiple schools in the district were in deplorable physical condition. The district worked hard to give voice and empowerment to many diverse city groups. As a result, a massive "bricks and mortar" bond issue was developed and presented to the public that concentrated solely on improving the infrastructure within the district. Although many said it would never succeed, the bond passed last year with more than 70 percent of the vote. As district stakeholders celebrated the success for the obvious facilities improvements it would bring, they also celebrated something of equal importance. The vote was also one of support for the new culture, climate, and visionary leadership they were seeing displayed within their district.

As evidenced in Dallas, there are many management skills necessary to facilitate the smooth organization and operation of facilities, budgets, personnel, and safety in learner-focused schools. If the devil is really in the details, here is where he often raises his ugly head with both new and experienced principals.

Manage the Organization

First, let's look at the distinctions between managing the organization from managing its operations. In our instance, *the organization is the school,* so when we talk about managing it, we are referring to the structural framework. Conversely, when we discuss the operations of the school, we mean the daily activities necessary to keep the school *operating* smoothly and efficiently.

Whereas Standard 1 is about the visionary leadership of the principal, Standard 3 is about the "nuts and bolts" of leadership and business management. For example, one district could have an organizational structure of elementary schools with PreK–5, Grades 6–8 in middle school, and Grades 9–12 in high school. That is their organizational structure. Another equally good district could have PreK–2 located in early childhood centers, Grades 3 and 4 in elementary schools, Grades 5 and 6 in intermediate schools, Grades 7 and 8 in middle schools, Grade 9 as a separate school, and Grades 10–12 located within high schools. This would be an entirely different organizational structure, but it is what they have chosen to implement. Similar examples could be exhibited within specific school contexts. One school could have self-contained classes, whereas another with the same grade levels could chose to have their students rotate between content-specific classes. The exact chosen structure is not the issue as long as it is soundly research-based and focused on creating a culture and climate that enhances the success of every student. It's a matter of choice, which is totally fine *as long as* the decisions to organize the schools, in whatever manner, are based on data with attention to equity, effectiveness, and efficiency criteria. The results will evidence themselves in student performance. Again, everything must be focused on student learning needs. There are no exceptions. Thus, the primary role of administrators with regard to Standard 3 is to make certain the organization, operations, and resources provided for the school are utilized with equity, effectiveness, and efficiency in mind.

Decisions regarding the learning environment, culture, and climate of the school should be made through applying appropriate models and principles of organizational development and management. These same principles should also be used for any other decisions regarding human resources, fiscal operations, facilities, legal issues, scheduling, technology, and equipment. To do this, the principal must make certain everyone knows and understands his or her job responsibilities and that an accountability system is in place. These are excellent starting points for you as you work with your Induction Partnership team. The experienced administrators on your team have been around the block repeatedly with these issues. They can facilitate your growth by asking you reflective questions to guide you in the right direction as you search for answers. They also have the experience of knowing people and networks of vertical and horizontal educators to put you in contact with those who have the expertise in the areas you need and can provide you formative as well as summative feedback.

It is your responsibility to connect the action plans developed with the vision, goals, and resources needed for the effective management of the school. There is more to the management of the school than school finance, although that is a big component. You must also incorporate the faculty, staff, and school community in ways to align human and material resources with student learning through curriculum and instruction. Remember, human resources come in multiple fashions. There are the paid employees of the school and the vast untapped resources of community members, clubs, businesses, churches, social service agencies, and so forth that can be solicited and utilized to broaden student opportunities and perspectives. Most of these do not cost money. They do cost the time it will take you and others to develop relationships with them, letting them know what assets they can be to your school. I will discuss the development of these relationships further in Chapter 6. As principal, you will lead faculty and staff in developing partnerships with families and others in the community. Always remember that everything you do and the work you do with others is for the purpose of a single goal. That goal is to promote student achievement in any way possible.

Manage Operations

As discussed in Chapter 3, all resources and their procurement must be aligned with the vision of the school. Not all resources are purchased. Many things are donated by a variety of people. School volunteer programs are becoming, and should become, more and more effective and popular. Faculty, staff, and community members were involved in the development, articulation, and implementation of the vision. They should continue to be involved in setting school priorities, conducting operations, and using diverse methods to address data-driven decision making, build consensus, communicate with each other, and resolve interpersonal conflicts.

Whenever you empower more than one person to be involved in decision making, it is inevitable that there will eventually be differences of opinion. To a certain extent, this is good. Communicating with one another, as well as with families and community groups, is also good. We don't want everyone thinking and feeling exactly the same way. Where is the diversity in that? As in the example of the stagnant pond, we need new ideas to help us broaden our perspectives. But when differences of opinion are no longer helpful, constructive, and enlightening, tensions can arise that create problems in the organization. This is not a good thing. Therefore, the principal, with the help of the Induction Partnership team, must address specific ways to resolve conflicts and bring perspectives into a consensus that is acceptable for the stakeholders and, even more important, the best thing for students. The operations of the school are managed effectively when there is an understanding and application of legal tenets that encourage and support academic equity as well as supporting effective and efficient facilities.

The issue of school safety is one that has everyone concerned in our uncertain times. A generation ago students practiced duck-and-cover drills in addition to regular weather-related and fire drills. Through the years, duck-and-cover drills were dropped, and now today's students would not know what they were.

With the increase of school violence and the threat of terrorist threats, there has been recent discussion of reviving duck-and-cover drills as a part of Emergency and Crisis Management Systems. It is sad to think that young students go to school and need to have any thought cross their minds about terrorists or others trying to kill them. This is sad, but true. It is even sadder that we now have to teach our nation's young people survival techniques for potential catastrophic events that could happen in schools. The effective new principal does not forget that these bizarre happenings can occur on their schools. We must all be ever diligent and careful, be prepared, have an Emergency and Crisis Management Plan, practice it, and then pray we never have to use it.

Manage Resources

To manage the organizational and operational facets of the school effectively, it is essential to have appropriate resources. One of the most forgotten resources to budget for and manage is time. It doesn't matter if your teachers have every material imaginable, if they do not have time to learn how to use it, it isn't going to do them a lot of good. Teachers can have the best intentions in the world, but if they do not have time to interact with others, to plan collaboratively, or to meet with parents to discuss the progress of their children, again, resources on their shelves won't make a lot of difference. Therefore, it is vital to budget for the creative utilization of time for yourself and others.

No matter how well long-range and strategic plans are developed and implemented, there are usually things that come up that necessitate more resources than most schools actually have. It is crucial to have solid relationships with others in the community that can help you procure the things you need for teachers to do their jobs effectively. The creative ideas people can come up with when they put their heads together to solve problems or procure resources are truly amazing. Sometimes the resources are not monetary in nature: it's nice to have someone who will actually dress up as Mary and bring a lamb to school for Storybook Character Day. It's nice when someone provides a cow costume so you can dress up as the Cow That Jumped Over the Moon and go from classroom to classroom talking to students about setting high goals and expectations. There are parents who will bring live chickens to school to show that different types produce different kinds of eggs. They will also bring example eggs to school as well. The possibilities are limitless, but the point remains the same. Principals and other educators must develop relationships that facilitate the creative procurement of new and different resources that engage and enhance student learning.

In addition to budget issues, human resources are also a tremendous part of the role of the principal. In fact, many experienced and wise administrators say that the way you work with people can be your greatest asset or your strongest weakness, depending on your personality, people skills, and other facets of conflict resolution and team and consensus building. People will give you the biggest headaches and also the greatest joys. Therefore, you must have, and continuously develop, your skills in job analysis, supervision, recruitment, selection, retention, professional development, and appraisal of all staff members. In states with collective bargaining, this can sometimes be a challenge. If your state is a collective bargaining state, you will need additional training on what to say and do as well as what *not* to say and do. Usually districts provide this training and have their own specified procedures and regulations for it.

Finally, principals must have a working knowledge of technological tools for resource procurement, utilization, and management. Technology on both the school and district level has provided instant accessibility with diverse resources around the world. This can and should be utilized both in classrooms and in the office. The office will use technology for business procedures, managerial purposes, and scheduling while classrooms and libraries can use the Internet to put the world into the hands of students and teachers. In the Information Age, accessibility is the key to new opportunities for all learners for the entire school community. In the end, all resources must be collaboratively planned for, procured, and utilized to maximize student productivity.

PROBLEM-BASED LEARNING

Plop Plop, Fizz Fizz, Oh, What a Relief It Is . . .

Robert Graham Alternative High School was founded to facilitate at-risk students who for various reasons had not been successful in their regular high schools. Students included young mothers, others who were forced to work for survival or to help their families make ends meet, those who had lost interest in school or graduating, those who could not wait to graduate but who were behind academically, and those who felt they did not fit in anywhere. Appealing aspects of Graham Alternative included the flexible hours, self-paced program, and missionary zeal of the teachers who were there by personal choice. The faculty and staff at Graham were committed to helping these young people find their way and obtain a high school diploma.

When Graham was originally formed, it was a cooperative effort between the Mountain Creek school district and six smaller ones. Mountain Creek charged the other districts on a per-student basis for their students to be able to attend Graham. The smaller districts were also required to provide their own students' transportation. In this manner, it was more economically feasible for the smaller districts to pay Mountain Creek for their students to attend than it was for them to develop their own alternative programs and facilities. As time passed, however, Mountain Creek regularly raised the tuition until, one by one, all of the other districts made different arrangements for their students. This left Mountain Creek bearing the full financial responsibility for the facility and its programs.

Because of these increasing fiscal concerns, the superintendent of Mountain Creek wanted to close the school or come up with another way to organize and manage the operations and resources necessary for the alternative school to survive. Therefore retiring teachers and staff were not replaced, and although this saved money up front, it placed an increased burden on the remaining educators who picked up the load. Students at Graham, they reasoned, were nontraditional learners who needed unique instructional strategies, intense individual instruction, and counseling to deal with their various personal issues. Unfortunately, Graham was not allowed to have a full-time counselor. Speaking strictly from a financial vantage point, the superintendent said there were not enough students at the school to merit a full-time counselor. The faculty countered that these students had problems or they wouldn't be at Graham in the first place. Obviously, the school and district leadership were addressing the needs of Graham Alternative from entirely different perspectives.

As time went by, the teachers were totally frustrated by overwork and lack of appreciation. They believed that no matter what they did or how hard they worked for the students, nothing they did was valued. Worse, they felt the students were not valued by a system that focused on traditional learners at the expense of nontraditional ones. Faculty and student morale and school climate were low, and they were afraid their school would be closed. Numerous students began talking about dropping out because the school would probably close in any event. "What is the use of continuing to come?" they reasoned.

The principal, Jose Valiant, felt awkward about the entire situation. He knew he must remain objective throughout the emotional process. He also knew he must show loyalty to the superintendent or he could lose his job. But the truth was, he agreed with the teachers. It did appear that the elimination of Graham was targeted as a major budget cut without appropriately considering the needs of these atypical learners. The bottom line appeared to be entirely financial. The management, operations, and resources needed to keep Graham Alternative open were not viewed as being cost effective to the district. Jose knew someone had to come up with a plan or the Robert Graham Alternative High School truly would close. The ultimate losers in this tragedy would be current and future students. Through this, eventually the community as a whole would lose as well.

Because the faculty and staff at Graham Alternative were small, Jose reasoned the thing to do was to turn their private "Woe is us" attitude into something positive. The thing to do, he reasoned, was to focus all their energy into coming up with a fiscally responsible school reorganization and management plan that would also met the needs of the students. Regardless, morale was so low, he wasn't certain he could persuade others to buy into his idea. Nonetheless, he adopted a philosophy of "Nothing ventured, nothing gained." He called a meeting to discuss the idea of developing a reasonable solution that would involve and benefit the community. Jose shared the idea with his superintendent and other administrators. Although the superintendent expressed skepticism over the idea's likelihood of success, Jose was given permission to implement the plan.

The afternoon Jose met with the teachers, he explained his idea of their working together to create a new fiscal and operational plan that they all could share and support. His model was to take site-based decision making beyond district guidelines. He was willing to open all facets of the budget, state and district regulations, and any other data they needed as they attempted to develop a plan to save their school. To Jose's vast surprise, the teachers loved his idea. They even suggested taking it a step further. Because Graham Alternative was a small school and the students felt as if their opinions didn't matter, the teachers suggested allowing students to elect representatives to work on the development of the proposed new model. In this way, they could directly connect teaching economics, the democratic process, and governmental policy and process. They reasoned that Graham students learned more appropriately by using a constructivist approach and actively doing something than simply studying the same concepts from a text. This would be a good way to tie theory to practice, make learning authentic, and let students see the impact their work could have. They also invited parents, spouses, and community members to become involved in the process. Many of these people, though not all, enthusiastically said they would love to help. None of them wanted the school to close. Parents were thrilled to have their sons and daughters in a place where they felt cared for and nurtured rather than rejected. They very much wanted their children to continue to have the opportunity to get a high school diploma, even if Graham Alternative didn't have proms or pep rallies. The biggest goal for the families was for these young adults to become high school graduates and go to college or enter the work force as educated citizens. Without a diploma, they reasoned, these kids were going to have a long, tough life.

Of course, there was a downside. What if the combined school-community partnership couldn't come up with a plan? Were they prepared to face disappointment and failure? What if they were able to come up with suggestions to make the school financially solvent, but the superintendent or school board rejected it? What if—perish the thought—the superintendent rejected their plan without ever showing it to the school board? What would happen then? Would any of them be able to handle the rejection and hurt?

Regardless, after much consideration, the team decided to go forward. Students enthusiastically rose to the occasion. Additional community and school volunteers were solicited to serve on the team. A student election was held to select their team representatives. They weren't exactly your "traditional" student body leaders. For all of them, it was the first time there were actively engaged in an election process. When they had been at Mountain Creek High School, they were totally disenfranchised from co-curricular and extracurricular activities. At Graham Alternative, things were different. Now they were actually a part of an election, campaigning for friends, and absorbed with their ideas of how to facilitate Graham Alternative staying open and becoming an even better place for learning.

Eventually the team came up with a reorganization plan that they were very proud of. The student representatives had risen to the occasion and provided regular insights and feedback to and from the rest of the school. Students participated in ongoing conversations about their ideas. Admittedly, some thought all of it was a waste of time and that nothing they did would have an impact. Others, however, felt differently. If nothing else, Jose reflected, at least people who cared were actively engaged in trying to develop a good plan to make a bad situation improve. Even better, they no longer had time to sing the "Woe Is Me Blues."

Finally, after many hours of meetings, ideas, brainstorming, research, and number crunching, the team finalized a plan that made them feel confident and excited. They truly believed if the superintendent and board would look at it with an open mind, they would see the plan could work.

After they got over their initial shock that the superintendent did, indeed, place their plan on the agenda to discuss in open session, the team had a celebration at their school. This encouraged the rest of the student body to attend the meeting. "Come!" they begged. "We need you there!"

Not a single student at Graham Alternative had ever attended a school board meeting. The very idea of any kind of authority figures either scared them to death or brought out their rebellious streaks. With the continual urging of their teachers and Jose, however, many agreed to come. "Showing your faces in the audience makes you real people instead of just names on a roster to the superintendent and board," their teachers told them. "We need you to come and support our school!"

So, come they did! Several student-mothers brought their babies and young children. Many students were able to get off from work but wore their fast food and other uniforms to the meeting to make apparent the extra efforts they had to undertake just to be able to attend school. It had the desired effect. Seeing was believing. The superintendent did an excellent job articulating and explaining the plan to the board. The board asked interested and intelligent questions, while Jose, the faculty, staff, students, babies, and parents sat listening and waiting with their hearts in their throats and pulses racing.

After considerable discussion of pros, cons, finances, accountability, and other issues back and forth, the board voted to accept the team's restructuring plan for Graham Alternative School. The Graham crowd jumped up and applauded. Some people cried. The press took pictures and interviewed people for local media. The school was going to stay open—and serve the students even better than before. How did they know it would be better? Because they created the plan together, brainstorming potential solutions to every conceivable problem until they had covered every obstacle. They were proud of their school. The students learned that the democratic process could work if they became educated to the right methods and activities toward a cause they strongly believed in. Long live Robert Graham Alternative School and the students it serves.

REFLECTIVE ANALYSIS

Manage the Organization

1. Compare and contrast the distinctions between operational and organizational management.

2. You are a member of the partnership team that just created the successful Graham Alternative restructuring plan. Describe the *organizational* management plan presented to the board.

3. Part of what the superintendent and board appreciated about the plan was its system for assessment and accountability. Describe an assessment and accountability system for organizational management at an alternative school. In what ways, if any, would this be the same or different as at a regular high school?

4. Brainstorm, describe, and discuss variables that could potentially be different in the management of a traditional versus an alternative school.

5. Design a model organizational format for a secondary alternative school that targets innovative design, curriculum, instructional techniques, and flexible hours focused on student needs.

Manage Operations

1. You are a member of the partnership team that just created the successful Graham restructuring plan. Describe the *operational* management plan presented to the board. Be specific about the distinctions between organizational and operational management.

2. Describe the plan's assessment and accountability system for operational management. Be specific about the distinctions between organizational and operational assessment and accountability.

3. Considering the limited financial resources in most schools, describe an operational model that decentralizes responsibilities and creates autonomy.

4. Develop an accountability system for the operational autonomy and responsibility model described in Point 3.

5. Create an ideal operational management plan for your school. What specific improvements could be made to your operational system?

Manage Resources

1. Compare and contrast resource management with organizational and operational management.

2. You are a member of the partnership team that just created the successful Graham restructuring plan. Describe the *resource* management plan presented to the board.

3. Describe the plan's assessment and accountability system for *resource* management.

4. Describe an ideal model for budget development, procurement, utilization, and accountability. How could faculty empowerment and accountability contained in the model be facilitated?

5. Create an ideal resource management plan for your school. What specific improvements could be made in budget development, procurement, and utilization?

APPLICATION OF THE
INDUCTION PARTNERSHIP MODEL

1. Looking at the first six Educational Leadership Constituent Council standards, identify three goals for each standard to help Jose develop and grow as an administrator for Robert Graham Alternative High School.

2. In what ways could the Induction Partnership Model be applied at Robert Graham to help Jose succeed? Elaborate on the basic model to create an individualized growth plan for Jose. In what specific ways could Jose develop his skills in managing the organization, operations, and resources of the school in a way that promotes a safe, efficient, and effective learning environment?

3. Identify and elaborate on strategies each of the following stakeholders could partner together to help Jose meet his goals for effective organizational, operational, and resource management:

- Self
- Mentor
- District
- University or certifying agency
- Business–school community partnerships
- Family and friends

4. What resources will be needed for each participant to fulfill his or her responsibilities? Utilizing all stakeholders, how could these resources best be solicited and utilized?

5. Develop accountability measures and a time line per goal to assure growth and measurement are occurring as planned in a proactive and timely manner. Determine as a team how these issues can be brought before the group on a continuing basis to ensure development is taking place.

6. Design an ideal application of the Induction Partnership Model to help you grow in your current situation in regard to managing the organization, operations and resources of the school in a way that promotes a safe, efficient, and effective learning environment.

CONCLUSIONS

For schools to run efficiently, effectively, and with equitable resources, the principal must bring both a global and a specific perspective to school leadership and management. The details of budget development and utilization for the benefit of effective teaching and learning are absolutely necessary. Without appropriate resources, these things cannot take place. Principals must therefore find creative ways to procure everything needed for teachers to teach, for students to learn, and for everyone to be safe. Often this will involve the building of firm relationships and partnerships with diverse community groups with interests in your school.

ACTIVITIES FOR ADMINISTRATOR INDUCTION AND PROFESSIONAL DEVELOPMENT

The Standards-Based "Sweet 16" Induction Developmental Activities

- Utilize collaborative school planning, procurement, management, and spending of the school budget and other resources.
- Document all budget expenditures.
- Join administrative organizations that provide current research regarding theory, best practices, legislation, and policies.
- Regularly walk around and the interior and perimeter of the school building(s), using careful observation to ensure school safety and efficiency. Encourage others to do likewise.
- Create an assessment team to evaluate and update school safety drill procedures including fire, severe weather, and crisis management.
- Encourage attendance by faculty, staff, parents, and others at local, state, and national conferences concerning student safety and crisis.
- Provide management training for teachers concerning assessing, interpreting, and analyzing testing data in a technological format.
- Collaboratively assess school and staff professional growth needs. Identify and provide a plan for efficient support resources to provide development in those areas.
- As a school, identify inefficient programs as well as plans to modify or eliminate them.
- Collaboratively develop, analyze, and evaluate the existing school needs assessment survey. Utilize school needs in the development of the school vision and attainment goals.
- Form a budget planning committee of diverse stakeholders to provide recommendations to align available resources and potential alternative funding options to meet school goals.
- Cultivate partnerships with diverse community organizations. Together, brainstorm possible resources other than money by which the school and the organizations can mutually benefit.
- Facilitate the development and implementation of a consistent schoolwide discipline management plan that is ethical, fair, and developmentally appropriate to meet varying student needs.
- Provide teachers and staff the opportunity to attend professional development activities to enrich student learning.
- Facilitate training on budget planning and alignment of resources with the goals and vision of the school.
- Facilitate team building and conflict resolution strategies to maximize organizational productivity.

6 I Have to Work With *Them?*

Pretend that every single person you meet has a sign around his or her neck that says, "Make Me Feel Important." Not only will you succeed in sales, you will succeed in life.

—Mary Kay Ash

STANDARD 4

Candidates who complete the program are educational leaders who have the knowledge and ability to promote the success of all students by collaborating with families and other community members, responding to diverse community interests and needs, and mobilizing community resources.

TOP TEN THINGS ADMINISTRATORS WISH THEY HAD KNOWN BEFORE ENTERING THE PRINCIPALSHIP

Principals must

1. Be visible and actively involved in the community on behalf of the school.

2. Keep their eyes and ears open and responsive to school and community concerns and potential "hot spots" that could develop.

3. Be fully cognizant of all legal and familial child custody issues.

4. Network with other educational professionals, community members, and civic, social, and religious organizations that can benefit student needs.

5. Be solicitous, respectful, and tolerant of all stakeholders.

6. Be aware that some parents do not know or understand their children's educational needs. You must guide them.

7. Learn to listen empathetically to create trust and facilitate partnerships for the benefit of all students.

8. Develop practical expertise in interpersonal sensitivity and conflict resolution in working with parents or other caregivers during difficult student discipline issues.

9. Spend interactive time getting to know the interests, needs, and culture of families in the school community.

10. Always be watching for people or groups with whom you can partner to maximize student success.

PHILOSOPHICAL FRAMEWORK

Ah, the glorious redwood trees of California! What a grand testimony to nature to see these giant trees and hear the wind as it blows through their branches. Tall and majestic, they represent the American spirit to many of us as they sway but never break though winter winds pound them from the westward coast. In awe people repeatedly wonder how trees can grow that large in height, diameter, and majesty.

Botanists tell us that their strength is underground, where it cannot be seen. The root systems of the giant redwoods have become interwoven with one another. Instead of the roots strangling each other, they blend to provide unseen strength for all the trees. It is a perfect example of a true gestalt because the sum of the root systems creates trees that are stronger than any of them would be individually. When the storm clouds come, the unseen root systems interlock, support, and bind the trees together. They are stronger together than apart.

This is exactly the type of seen and unseen collaborative partnerships we need to be creating in our schools. The days of each school operating as an independent unit are gone. With all the societal pressures surrounding us today, we must work smarter rather than harder. Forming teams with families, community members, and organizations has become an

I Have to Work With *Them?* ● 83

essential component in responding to community interests and needs as well as mobilizing resources to fulfill them.

This is a staggering task even for experienced principals, but for newcomers it can be totally overwhelming. As they struggle to hold the walls of the school together, the last thing they have on their minds or think they have time for is venturing into the community to create partnerships. It's about all they can do to develop relationships inside the school, much less outside of it. So, what are they supposed to do now?

Collaborate With Families and Other Community Members

In Chapter 5 on Standard 3, we talked about the importance of building relationships with families and other community groups for the purpose of providing necessary financial and, often even more important, nonfinancial resources for the school. The seven Educational Leadership Constituent Council (ELCC) standards were not developed to be solitary issues but should be integrated. The real life of a principal is integrated, and therefore when a principal goes into the community to solicit resources to help the school attain its vision and goals, this is a combination of Standard 3 (organizational management, operations, and resource management) as well as Standard 4 (collaborative partnerships). Regardless of which standard this applies to, it is critical to the success of the school as well as that of the administrator to be actively engaged in working with families and the community to procure their talents, skills, knowledge, and cultural base as well as resources.

To do this, we must start from the inside and work outward. Each student at the school has some variation of a family. The place to begin creating partnerships is to start with the families of students, creating trust with them and the community by building relationships. Relationship building is the primary tool to success in school or most other organizational leaderships. Administrators can do that by becoming actively involved in diverse types of community activities that reflect the interests and values that are important to them. Notice I didn't say to become involved in just the ones of interest to the principal personally but rather with things that are important to the people and neighborhoods the school serves. This could lead you to some unique places, but if that is where the people go and it is safe and moral, it is where you go. Only by getting directly involved with the community can you get to know the parameters of their world, what motivates them, as well as where their values and concerns lie. Likewise, you are simply another authority figure from the "establishment," someone who maybe should or maybe should not be trusted until they get to know you. Trust is built. It can also be destroyed too easily, so lay your foundation securely. It will lead you through any rough spots down the road. Getting to know and become known in the community is not a frill to be done as you have time, but a strong focus from the day you begin your job. To develop communication and partnerships takes more than inviting families and community members into the school. It takes going out into their world to get to know them as individuals and groups to lay the foundation of the vision of the school and how you can work together to optimize success for every student regardless of ability or disability.

Individual schools as well as the district as a whole are a huge and integral component of the greater community. Schools that are perceived poorly affect the entire town economically, politically, and socially. When schools thrive and are well perceived, the community will thrive as well. If the schools do not thrive, the community will be adversely affected. Any realtor will tell you that customers regularly ask about the quality of the schools as they are looking at homes in various neighborhoods. Likewise, chambers of commerce and economic development foundations also stress the value of quality schools as a recruiting tool when they solicit new businesses into the community. We do not want to get into anything that affects the school, district, or town negatively; therefore we must do everything we can think of to create positive relationships with all community stakeholders. Based on the belief that parents really do care about the best interests of all students as well as their own, utilize them in as many school decision-making processes as possible just as you did when developing your school vision, goals, and strategies for attainment (Standard 1). In this manner, the success of all students as well as the reputation of the school are enhanced.

Your outreach should not be limited to parents and others directly involved with the school but should also extend to business, religious, political, service organizations, and the media. Too often it seems that the media is more interested in selling papers or advertising than in providing a broad perspective on a diverse array of positive things taking place at the school. Because this is a shame and has a direct relationship to public perception, it is essential that positive relationships be developed with the media. One way to do this is to oversaturate them with invitations to positive activities and with press releases and pictures of students and other stakeholders actively involved in interesting projects, contests, awards, and any other enticing thing you and others within and outside of the school can think of. Be especially solicitous of the media as you show off the many great things you are proud of at your school. If you establish strong bonds and relationships with them up front, it's like putting money in the bank. Sooner or later something absurd could happen at your school, and when it does your personal credibility as well as that of the school will have an influence on the way the media portray the incident. Do not ignore the press. Make them your new best friends.

Together with your faculty and others, develop a comprehensive plan that addresses improving community relations and those with the media. To find out what will appeal to people, ask them. Invite all types of people representing diverse segments of the population to come in, be a part of the team, and provide significant input as to what is of need or interest as well as how to address it. These same issues are important with all decision-making processes.

Because you are seeking formative, and later summative, input from all sorts of people, ask them what the positive and not so positive experiences are that they have had with various health, social, and other community service agencies. Together come up with strategies by which the school can serve as a facilitator and "point person" to help families connect with all the services they need. When the needs of families are met, the needs of students are better obtained. Everyone knows from their studies of Benjamin Bloom's (1956, 1982) taxonomy that until basic human needs are met, they cannot optimally learn or achieve. This is a large part of the rationale for the Federal Free and Reduced Lunch and Breakfast Programs. The other part is that it is a disgrace in the vast wealth of our nation for any child to be hungry at school or anywhere else. Often young people go without food, health services, and other necessities simply because all the right pieces are not in place to facilitate this happening. Because people are busy or perhaps lack true, personalized concern, no one has taken the time to *help* these people pull the pieces together. Yes, we realize you cannot be the personal social service provider for every student in your school. With the help of site-based decision-making commitments and frameworks as well as your Induction Partnership team, however, plans can be laid, advice and direction provided, and facilitation can occur to help students have what they need to be successful.

To know how to facilitate these services, principals must know how to use public information and research or they won't know how to help anyone. This is particularly true with new principals who may or may not be familiar with the area or town. Again, this is why becoming involved *outside* the school can be as important as inside. Principals must continuously be studying, analyzing, and watching any issues and trends that may affect students and learning. When you think about it, exactly what could be going on in the community or the world that would *not* affect learning? Did September 11 impact student learning? You bet it did. It changed our entire way of life. If you don't believe that, walk into any airport today and experience the increased security. Every change in society, every nuance, every conversation at home, on the streets, or anywhere else has a direct or indirect impact on student learning. For these reasons the principal must be astutely aware of current events, trends, and potential issues to be able to think ahead proactively, involve others, and create plans for how to address them.

Finally, as a principal you must always be working to improve your communication skills to be able to articulate clearly everything that is going on at school, for what purposes, and how it will enhance student learning. If something is not enhancing student learning, get rid of it. It serves no useful purpose. Just because it has always been done is not a good enough reason to keep it when it is a waste of time. To do this, you will constantly need to utilize your knowledge and communication skills for the purpose of creating positive and productive collaborative partnerships with families, businesses, civic and government affiliations, social service agencies, religious groups, and higher education.

Remember, though, that a partnership is not a one-way street. It is not only a matter of what they can do for the school but also what can the school do for them. The answers to both of these questions are as limitless as the creativity of the people involved. Keep in mind that there is a lot more to partnerships than money and other tangible resources. True partnerships are like marriages. They are affairs of the heart and work both ways. Working with so many groups can provide endless opportunities for service learning and social justice projects that will teach civic responsibility for students of all ages. In so doing, we are teaching our students so much more than academics. We are teaching them that life is definitely not all about receiving. It is about giving of ourselves to help others. In the end, isn't that what civic responsibility as well as life is all about?

Respond to Community Interests and Needs

As discussed earlier, it is critically important for new and experienced principals to be actively engaged in the community. We also discussed the importance of being in continuous interaction with all different aspects of the community and bringing people together to problem solve on virtually every issue that affects teaching and learning.

But sometimes when this happens, conflict can be the result. It's a natural occurrence if you really are bringing in all kinds of different perspectives. Not everyone in the community is going to want to hold hands with everyone else while singing "Kumbaya." That's why it is called having different perspectives. Sometimes they are polar opposites! Sometimes there are deep-seated issues that go way back to a time before you ever knew this school existed that have created situations in which some people in the community truly do not like each other. In fact, they may hate each other and be exceedingly verbal about it. Why on earth would you, the new kid on the block, have any success bringing them together when they have hated each other for years?

Because you have the *future* in the palm of your hands in the form of our offspring, our students, our children, the *future* of our world. No other group has that. So capitalize on it.

Remember in Chapter 3 (Standard 1) when we talked about bringing vastly different people together to develop the school vision? This is the perfect place to begin pulling these people together. Before that point, do your homework. Lay your groundwork before they are in the same room together. When you initially invite them to be a part of the decision-making team, be honest and upfront about the purposes of what you are trying to do for the school, the students, and the community. Tell them you are asking them to make a *commitment* to lay aside personal differences with anyone else who may be involved for the purpose of our *common goal* of improving teaching and learning for every student *in our entire community.* The school is not the place for special interest groups to grind out their differences. While you are all there together, you are going to focus on one thing and one thing only: *How can we make this school better at this point in time by all of us working together?* Ask them to make this commitment before they agree to serve. Tell them they do not have to become best friends with their archenemies, but that you do expect, and the school deserves, their best and most focused behavior and work ethic to help the kids. If they can't do that, ask them nicely not to agree to serve. Then provide everyone copies of *Leadership and the Force of Love* (2002) by John R. Hoyle to read and reflect on the powerful influence of love and role-modeling on other people's lives.

Of course, along the way you have shared your personal vision with them and talked about the new path the school is going to take. You have stressed the major impact you and the faculty expect these potential initiatives to have on the greater school area as a whole, the individual needs of every student (Standard 2)—particularly those with special academic, physical, or psychological needs—and, finally, the pride of being a part of something so big and so exciting that it is going to leave a lasting legacy in their town. You have stressed what an honor it is not only for faculty and staff to have considered them good candidates but for them actually to have been selected and invited to serve. Now who could turn down your request for honorable and professional behavior when it is on the behalf of young people? If you find someone who will actually admit to that, call me. I want to visit with that person. We would have a few serious things to discuss, and I promise it wouldn't take me long to get my points across and leave them weeping in shame.

Once you actually have people willing to serve, it's time to get this motor running and provide an organizational framework. Before we can accurately identify community interests, needs, and their distinctions, we must develop, articulate, implement, and assess needs assessment research strategies and an operational plan appropriate to the context. We do this by considering the following:

- What are our exact purposes?
- What do we hope to achieve?
- What should our research tools include?
- To whom should surveys, interviews, and so on, be given?
- How will we analyze and use the results?
- What are we going to do with the results to improve school and community dynamics, relationships, and improve teaching and learning?
- How will we assess the process?

All of these are important questions. Your discussions should not be limited to these, however. They should include as many relevant issues as you can brainstorm together. Again, your opportunities are limitless as long as you can get diverse stakeholders to agree to set everything else aside and strictly focus on what can be done to improve teaching and learning such that *every* student, including those with special needs, can maximize their learning and productivity.

If you can bring so many people from diverse backgrounds together on a regular basis to talk about all the issues you identify collectively, you will have taken a *major* step toward creating relationships and partnerships that focus on improved student success. As time goes by and the group generates success, if we are very, very lucky, the synergy created in this collaborative diverse partnership of stakeholders will have spin-off effects in the rest of the community. With a little more luck, civic dynamics can improve, which can result in greater productivity and growth in any number of areas.

Then people will get on their knees and beg you to quit your job as principal and run for president of the United States as a member of the "For the Future" party. Because the popular political parties often can't manage to come to a reasonable consensus, we just thought we would create our own "For the Future" party. When they ask you to run, you can say with a perfectly straight face, "No, thanks. I'm content within my personal mission of creating community and school partnerships that help students and society have an opportunity for a better tomorrow. I think I'll just stay here and remain dirt poor. But thank you for your offer of immense wealth and fame. I really do appreciate it."

Mobilize Community Resources

All right, I admit it. You may not be asked to run for president after all. Shucks. Ideally, though, now that you have everyone focused on improving life and society through the global education of children, it is time to mobilize community resources. I have always liked the way the ELCC used the term "mobilize" here. Somehow it makes me feel as if we are sending in the marines to blitz the situation. Frankly, I've seen more than one state of affairs that could use a little blitzing, and some of those have been in schools. So what are we as a team going to do about it?

Mobilizing resources is directly connected to Standard 3 on procuring and managing resources. At this point, however, we have worked together to research and identify school and community interests and needs. We have multiple stakeholders involved in the process. We remember that people support what they help create and congratulate ourselves on our foresight for involving so many people that usually want to tear each other's eyes out. For the first time ever, they are agreeing on something. They are agreeing to improve the educational experience of students in their midst. They have come to a common understanding that what is best for the kids is what is best for everyone, regardless of race, culture, creed, or handicapping condition. Our focus has now shifted not just to identifying needs and concerns, but mobilizing resources to address them. The future and dignity of every student is at risk here which makes the stakes very, very high.

Now is the time, together with the team, to solicit services within the community to help resolve problems at the school, nurture student success, and reach those goals we set together. As volunteers and other resources and projects begin in school, now is the perfect time to utilize youth services and other public resources through projects that integrate service learning and social justice issues. Students should and must learn that they have to give back to the community (e.g., through service learning, community service, civic internships, etc.). Remember the social service agencies we discussed earlier? We must utilize those connections as well as school resources to respond and serve the community. They are excellent starting points from which to develop arrangements for students to be able to provide service to others in a safe, coordinated, and structured manner.

In a partnership relationship, both sides give and take. In the model described here, community members give of their expertise and resources to help the school succeed. In like manner, students give back to the community through service learning, volunteer work, and internships that teach civic responsibility and social justice. The responsibility of the principal does not stop here, however. As principal, you must always be looking to the future, staying abreast of current events on the local, state, national, and international levels for anything that might affect student learning. The team you have assembled should never stop meeting and working. Their roles are never complete. It is a long-term commitment because we will always continue to look for new ways to address community needs and concerns, integrate with the community, and find new ways to identify and obtain whatever resources are necessary to reach the goals of the school. We continue to look for ways to help teachers teach and students learn. That's now the official platform of the For the Future political party. Too bad the parties we already have aren't listening. They have a few things to learn about collaboration and partnerships. Maybe they should read our book. What do you think? I know! Maybe *I'll* run for president from the For the Future party. Until his death, my precious father, Lee Litchfield (1904–1987), used to tell me that to whom much is given, much is expected. One time he gave away my bicycle to a child who "needed it more than you." My bicycle! He gave away my bicycle! But that is the kind of person he was.

We have too many people today who have never learned that to give to or serve others is a blessing. Maybe they didn't have my daddy. Maybe they just weren't listening to what they were being taught. Maybe they just weren't taught! These people live in isolated worlds and do not understand, or do not care to understand, the situations of others who are not so fortunate. It is our job to teach civic responsibility to every student, regardless of his or her own circumstances. There are few things in life that can enhance self-esteem and have a positive effect on learning and life as giving of yourself to others. So while we are mobilizing community resources to help the school, we must also be teaching and requiring our students to give back likewise to the community. They will mature and have a better understanding of life because of the things they do to help others. It is a lesson my father taught me. He gave away my bicycle, you know.

Now let's read about Florence Turner and the work she did at Jesse Jai McNeil, Jr. Elementary School. If ever there was an impassioned educator, it was Florence. Read on!

PROBLEM-BASED LEARNING

It's Been a Hard Day's Night

As far back as Florence Turner could remember, she had a passion and yearning in her heart for the underrepresented and oppressed people of society. As a young African American, she had been active in many forms of volunteer, service learning, and outreach programs. There was no doubt in her mind that she would become a teacher. Throughout college she associated with other young people with the same goals and vision. After college, she began her teaching career, always focusing her energies on low socioeconomic, inner-city urban schools. Through the years, Florence's teaching background was rich in cultural contexts and varied experiences. The one thing that never wavered, though, was her strong passion to assist the downtrodden and to help others see life with new perspectives. Her engaging personality and her activism made her a robust community ally.

After teaching for ten years, Florence began to think that she could have a wider impact on society by becoming a school administrator. Her influence would then be multiplied beyond the students in her classroom to those throughout the entire school. In addition, because she was all ready well known among community service groups, by becoming a principal she could use those connections for the greater good of the school. Florence became excited about the possibilities as her mind raced ahead to all the things she could influence if she did, indeed, become a school level administrator. Someday, she reasoned, she possibly could also become a superintendent. She was filled with anticipation as she began graduate coursework to pursue her goal.

After graduating and becoming certified, Florence was quickly hired as an assistant principal at an intermediate school. In her three years in that position, her principal and others in the district acted as excellent mentors. She learned the inner workings, policies, and regulations that governed her school and district, as well as the intangible political influences that had direct bearing on decision making. Florence was always open to learning new things that would improve her school, but she felt frustrated by the bureaucratic layers that kept the school from being able to do immediately the things that needed to be done for teachers, students, families, and the community. She consoled herself with the knowledge that someday when she actually became the principal, her hands would be untied to some degree, and she would be able to get things done more quickly.

Sure enough, three years later Florence was assigned as principal of Jesse Jai McNeil, Jr. Elementary School. McNeil was a school with a rich mixture of student races, cultures, and religions. Florence was overjoyed and very excited about beginning her new venture; she felt McNeil was definitely the right place for her. Although her assistant principal experience had been at the intermediate level, she had taught elementary school for several years before entering administration. She was familiar with the state testing and accountability system and confident she could work within those parameters to effect positive change that would promote the success of students and their families.

When she began her new assignment Florence's natural enthusiasm and obvious commitment to the school diversity was contagious. There was a sense of renewal that quickly spread throughout the school. She immediately began outreach efforts within the school community and worked with various clubs, churches, and service organizations to help provide students with the things they needed to have an appropriate chance to succeed. If the nurse determined that a child had a vision problem and needed to see an eye doctor, but the family could not afford it, Florence made arrangements with the Lions Club to pay for it and then arranged the appointment. She was constantly in the community soliciting funds so that if a child could not afford to purchase books from the book fair or pay for a field trip or other school venture, he or she was never left out.

Florence did not limit her endeavors to fiscal issues. By constantly interacting with so many community members, she was able to facilitate the development of Big Sisters and Big Brother programs on the school. It broke her heart to see young children from single-parent homes who were struggling. Through Big Brother and Big Sister programs, many children were able to receive quality, one-on-one attention and mentoring from other adults in the community. She also worked with the high school that her students would eventually attend. She knew the principal and many of the faculty, so she solicited their help to form a partnership whereby at-risk high school students were partnered with elementary students who needed someone to listen to them read. The program proved vastly successful as young students' reading scores improved and the high school students benefited from the relationships they formed with the younger students and enjoyed the powerful effect of being needed and looked up to. Because her school had an extremely tight budget for the fine arts, Florence worked with the high school teachers to bring performers to McNeil. Again, they provided a "win-win" situation as the younger children were exposed to various forms of music and the arts, often imaging that they, too, could learn to sing or play an instrument and perform on stage. The high school students, needless to say, loved being released from class to go to the elementary school and perform. Their teachers also valued the positive exposure for their programs. In addition, the performances gave the students a chance to practice in front of live audiences.

Not stopping there, Florence went to local businesses to build Adopt a School programs that provided various resources, ranging from free tutoring, limited access to free photocopying, library resource donations, and appreciation lunches for faculty and staff. Some businesses provided nice prizes for teachers, whose names were drawn each month from those who had perfect attendance. Small incentives like these encouraged the faculty and staff to not be absent from work. Florence was strongly committed to having every teacher and paraprofessional present every day so that no student learning time was lost.

One of the best things Florence did, though, was to learn to listen. It was not something that came easily to her. Because she had so many ideas and such enthusiasm, it was difficult for her to recognize that other people had good ideas, too. It took her a while to realize and accept that others had been in this particular school community longer than she had and knew the neighborhood and its nuances better, and that even though she wanted to change the world, she couldn't do it overnight or without their help. She needed them, and they needed her. It took time and more than a few heartaches and frustrations before Florence came to this realization. She had to learn that passion and commitment were not enough. She had to learn to listen to parents, teachers, and the community rather than just ramming through in overdrive.

By the end of her first year at McNeil, Florence had learned a lot. She was proud of the strides McNeil had made in student performance and collaborative partnerships within the community. She was also completely worn out, however, both physically and emotionally. She felt drained of her resources and looked to the summer as a time to stare at the sky and do nothing. She knew the year had been hard on her family as well, because she spent so much time either at the school or involved in community endeavors. Looking back, she knew she had not spent the time she should have with her husband and family. She truly wished there had been some-one along the way who had had her best interest—and that of her school—at heart; she wished someone had counseled her to slow down, take it one step at a time, and not forget to give the culture change taking place within the school the time to grow and flourish. Florence took some hard knocks along the way as a number of people took her passion to be overbearing. "It's been a hard day's night this year," she told her husband late in the year. "Oh, the things I have learned. I just wish someone had told me to chill out and savor each day rather than trying to create so much change overnight. It would have been easier on everyone at home and at school. And it would have been far better for the students. I'm totally drained."

Florence resolved to strike a better balance the next year between her passion and zeal in helping others. She also promised herself that she would give the school and community time to absorb the forward momen-tum. She realized it doesn't matter how fast a train can go if it wrecks and runs off the track. She also promised to keep her eyes open for other begin-ning administrators who were traveling down her same high-speed path. She was determined to make sure she took the time to listen, then mentor and help steer them through the rough waters of their first year. She promised to try to help others avoid the pitfalls she encountered.

REFLECTIVE ANALYSIS

Collaborate With Families and Other Community Members

1. Discuss the pros and cons of a collaborative leadership style.

2. The implementation and utilization of collaboration in any form does not come naturally to some people. In what ways can collaborative skills be cultivated in beginning and experienced principals? In what ways would skill development be the same or different for beginning compared with experienced principals?

3. Identify and describe additional strategies to facilitate collaboration with families at McNeil Elementary.

4. Identify and describe additional strategies to facilitate collaboration between other community members and McNeil Elementary.

5. Reflecting on your own school situation, identify and plan strategies to facilitate collaboration with families and other community members for the benefit of students and learning.

Respond to Community Interests and Needs

1. Develop an assessment plan to identify and prioritize community interests and needs that could benefit students and families.

2. As the new principal of a school who has not reached out to identify community interests and needs, develop a framework for gathering staff and faculty input.

3. Your faculty is adamantly opposed to heightened community interactions. They say they work all day and grade all night, so they simply don't have time to add anything more to their plate. Then, too, it isn't safe to be out unaccompanied in this neighborhood. Further, they assert that they did not become teachers to also become social workers. Now what do you do?

4. Successful administrators proactively seek to identify potential community conflicts and possible solutions ahead of time. Role-play with a partner various scenarios and create solutions.

5. Reflecting on your own school situation, identify and plan strategies to respond to community interests and needs that will benefit students.

Mobilize Community Resources

1. Develop an assessment plan to identify potential community resources that could benefit students and families.

2. Develop a global school assistance plan that would align community resources with the vision and goals of your school.

3. Resources are more than just money. Which additional community assets can you identify and access to help your school achieve its goals and vision?

4. With the advancement of technology, schools have become global learning institutions. How could the Induction Partnership Model be used to identify and procure creative resources?

5. Reflecting on your own school situation, identify and plan strategies to mobilize community resources for the benefit of students.

APPLICATION OF THE INDUCTION PARTNERSHIP MODEL

1. Looking at the first six Educational Leadership Constituent Council standards, identify three goals per standard to help Florence develop and grow as an administrator for Jesse Jai McNeil, Jr. Elementary School.

2. In what ways could the Induction Partnership Model be applied at McNeil to help Florence succeed? Elaborate on the basic model to create an individualized growth plan for Florence that includes specific ways she could be assisted to develop in the areas of collaborating with families and other community members, responding to community interests and needs, and mobilizing community resources.

3. Identify and elaborate on strategies that each of the following stakeholders could implement to help Florence meet her goals of collaborating with families and other community members, responding to community interests and needs, and mobilizing community resources in a collaborative manner:

   - Self (in this case, Florence)
   - Mentor
   - District
   - University or certifying agency

- Business and school community leadership
- Family and friends

4. What resources will be needed for each participant to fulfill his or her responsibilities? Working with all stakeholders, how could these resources best be solicited and utilized?

5. Develop accountability measures for each goal to ensure that growth and assessment are occurring as planned in a proactive and timely manner. Determine as a team how these issues can be brought before the group on a continuing basis to ensure development is taking place.

6. Design an ideal application of the Induction Partnership Model to help you grow in your current situation in regard to collaborating with families and other community members, responding to community interests and needs, and mobilizing community resources.

CONCLUSIONS

Well, we have been around the block and back talking about the importance of developing collaborative partnerships with just about everyone in the school district—and sometimes beyond. There are no limitations. Everyone should be empowered in the success of a school somewhere. As many people as possible should be invited, solicited, or begged to become involved in *your* school. We want to involve people who look and think differently from us, as well as from each other, and who have diverse perspectives. We also know that to build a team and proactively practice conflict resolution, we must keep the focus strictly on how can we work together for the common goal of partnering to help *these* students at *this* school perform better academically as well as maturing as young civically responsible citizens. To do this, we must collaboratively develop, articulate, implement, and assess a plan to identify community and school needs and concerns as well as the resources necessary to address them. This is a never-ending process because we are ever vigilant for any external or internal forces that could affect student learning.

To that end we developed our own political party, but after due consideration I have decided not to run for president. I'm content within my personal mission of creating community and school partnerships that help students and society have an opportunity for a better tomorrow. I think I'll just stay a professor and remain dirt poor—but thank you for your offer of immense wealth and fame.

ACTIVITIES FOR ADMINISTRATOR INDUCTION AND PROFESSIONAL DEVELOPMENT

The Standards-Based "Sweet 16" Induction Developmental Activities

- In their homes and workplaces, discuss with parents, business, and other leaders to determine what the school can do for them and the local community.
- Work with local colleges and community education providers to develop and enhance partnerships such as dual credit and enrichment courses at the high school level.
- Present and promote the school as a bridge for all cultures by involving students, teachers, and community members in the development of a cultural fair where diverse constituencies can set up displays and lead discussions pertaining to their mores, backgrounds, traditions, ethnicities, and customs.
- Solicit opportunities for the community to add diverse resources, in addition to money, to the school. Multifaceted volunteerism should be targeted to enhance parental and neighborhood participation on school.
- Create and send a school newsletter to local businesses, parents, and other community leaders informing them of school events, programs, and progress toward the vision as well as soliciting continued input and participation.
- Host school-based community events in the evenings to allow parents and other stakeholders an opportunity to learn and participate in relevant educational issues and emerging themes.
- Create a multicultural committee of teachers and parents to create ways to display, discuss, and honor diverse groups represented in the school community.
- Develop, implement, and evaluate service learning strategies for students to facilitate and enhance community needs and volunteer programs.
- Provide day and evening opportunities for parents to come to the school and become involved in their child's education by developing "family activities" that can be done together.
- Develop programs and activities that integrate the neighborhood's traditions and culture into the school setting.
- Develop, implement, and evaluate school-based general education diploma and English as a second language programs for parents and other community members.

- Attend and be involved with community civic, cultural, and social activities (e.g., track meets, ball games, concerts, academic contest, art shows, etc.) that bring various members of the community together.
- Encourage school participation in community-sponsored events.
- Host a "recognition and appreciation day" for local businesses, parents, community members, families, and volunteers that have contributed time, work, and other resources to the school.
- Solicit the participation of parents, community members, businesses, and parents in school-based decision making.
- Invite community members and groups to participate in staff meetings and staff development days to discuss improvements that the school could make to improve its relationship and contributions to the neighborhood.

7 It May Be Legal, But Is It *Right?*

> *To know what is right and not to do it is the worst cowardice.*
>
> —Confucius

STANDARD 5

Candidates who complete the program are educational leaders who have the knowledge and ability to promote the success of all students by acting with integrity, fairness, and in an ethical manner.

TOP TEN THINGS ADMINISTRATORS WISH THEY HAD KNOWN BEFORE ENTERING THE PRINCIPALSHIP

Principals must

- Explicitly follow district and other professional codes of ethics.
- Always think of students first in decision making.
- Develop trust with their staff and school community.
- Listen to students, faculty, parents, and others, even if what they say doesn't make any sense.
- Remember that it is in their best interest not to react too quickly. Listen to all perspectives before making a judgment or decision. Just because it crosses your mind doesn't mean it must come out of your mouth.

- When making difficult decisions, always think about what is best for the students. Principals are not here to win a popularity contest. They cannot please everyone all the time.
- Learn how to handle sensitive issues. Thinking "out of the box" is a good thing when it addresses school and student needs. It is fine to not follow the status quo.
- Never assume that they are dealing with people who have the same understanding of professional behavior as they have.
- Know it is sometimes all right to call in the big dogs. Principals should keep their districts informed of potentially serious issues. Superintendents do not like to hear things for the first time from persons other than a principal. Don't spring surprises on superiors.
- Remember, it's lonely at the top. Create networking opportunities to support and encourage each other.

PHILOSOPHICAL FRAMEWORK

The beautiful area known as upstate New York is home of the United States Military Academy at West Point. Here many of our nation's best and brightest young men and women study to become the army military leaders of our future. If the first year doesn't kill them, they grow to become self-sufficient and confident strategists focused on being able to defend our country appropriately.

Nestled inside West Point is a beautiful old stone chapel where cadets of all faiths can worship together. Following graduation ceremonies each spring, the church and lawns are lined with young couples exchanging marriage vows, leaving the place where they have spent four grueling yet rewarding years and preparing to begin the next phase of the journey we call life.

In addition to worship and weddings in the chapel, the cadets also are taught something called the West Point Cadet Prayer (see Box 7.1). In it, they ask for guidance to choose "the harder right instead of the easier wrong, and never to be content with a half truth when the whole can be won." This may sound like a simple thing, but in truth it is very, very difficult. It may be the hardest thing any of us as humans ever confront. It is the highest standard of performance behavior imaginable.

The same is true in school leadership. Idealistic new administrators tell themselves they will always act with integrity and ethics, but the truth is that not every situation is black or white. There are contextual circumstances that affect the right decision in different situations. Therefore, sometimes being fair is not being consistent. This can create multiple

---

Box 7.1 West Point Cadet Prayer

WEST POINT CADET PRAYER

O God, our Father, Thou Searcher of human hearts, help us to draw near to Thee in sincerity and truth. May our religion be filled with gladness and may our worship of Thee be natural.

Strengthen and increase our admiration for honest dealing and clean thinking, and suffer not our hatred of hypocrisy and pretense ever to diminish. Encourage us in our endeavor to live above the common level of life.

Make us to choose the harder right instead of the easier wrong, and never to be content with a half-truth when the whole can be won. Endow us with courage that is born of loyalty to all that is noble and worthy, that scorns to compromise with the vice and injustice and knows no fear when truth and right are in jeopardy.

Guard us against flippancy and irreverence in the sacred things of life. Grant us new ties of friendship and new opportunity of service. Kindle our hearts in fellowship with those of a cheerful countenance, and soften our hearts with sympathy for those who sorrow and suffer.

Help us to maintain the honor of the Corps untarnished and unsullied and to show forth in our lives the ideals of West Point in doing our duty to Thee and to our country. All of which we ask in the name of Great Friend and Master of all. Amen.

---

problems for new administrators as well as for those all ready in the field. If there were a rule book of all the right and wrong things to do in dealing with people and things in a moral, ethical, and honorable way, it would make school leadership and life a lot easier to deal with.

Act With Integrity

Throughout this book we have talked about the importance of principals, regardless of their years of experience, making sure their walk matches their talk, not asking anyone to do something they would not do, and treating people with dignity and respect. That is what Standard 5 is all about. It brings together all the components of moral leadership into one standard framed around the critical elements of integrity, fairness, and ethics. In simple language, we could say "Treat people right." Unfortunately, the word "right" seems to have taken on an ambiguous meaning these days. There are "leaders" who treat others horribly then rationalize what they have done to make the other person sound like the bad guy. There are leaders who set other people up for failure. Then there are leaders who outright lie to reach their own goals, not caring what they are doing to other people or the organization in the meantime. To be completely honest, if we all think hard enough, we know we can come up with at least one person in a leadership position who is downright cruel, completely self-centered, plans his or her moves meticulously, and always seems to get away with it. These people leave the rest of the organization wondering exactly what is fair or honorable when the bad get rewarded while the hardworking keep their nose to the grindstone.

You will not be this way. You will always respect the rights of others, protect their confidentiality and dignity, and engage in honest interactions. As discussed in Chapter 5, schools are learning organizations. All organizations operate the most efficiently and effectively when their culture and climate are supportive and nurturing. This tone is set by the top leadership and permeates itself throughout the organization.

This is particularly true in schools where the principal is the focal point—the face and voice that people think of first when they consider a particular school or district. That person's persona and character are the first impression of the entire school. As principal you are the role model for the entire educational center. Like it or not, teachers, staff, students, parents, and many other community members are looking at you, watching you, seeing how you live your entire life not just at school but all around town. There are things you may have to give up doing as a school leader. It is all part of the total framework of what the community expects and deserves in its educational leaders. You will be a leader with integrity that people can trust and come to with their problems, concerns, or conflicts. You will help them find resolution because you lead your life in a manner that people can understand, trust, and respect. They do not have to love you, although it certainly helps, but they certainly must respect you.

Act Fairly

People sometimes confuse treating people consistently with treating them equitably and fairly. To treat everyone exactly the same in all circumstances is consistent. It does not, however, take into consideration the context of the situation as well as other circumstances. As an example, would we ask a student with a broken leg to run the 50-yard dash for a grade if everyone else has to do so? The orthopedist and I hope not. But that person should have to do something else or make up the 50-yard dash at an appropriate time. Although not consistent, this would be fair for the situation.

Other examples are Special Education laws. Notice that these are "laws," not suggestions. Individual Education Plans (IEPs) are designed to personalize instruction with modifications for a student to be successful even though the things they do and their assessment may be different from other students in the same class. Some people feel that is not consistent and therefore isn't right. On the other hand, is instructing the students on their individual levels what will best meet their unique learning needs? We hope so, because that is what IEPs were designed to do. It is fair and equitable, but not always consistent.

When, you ask, should you be consistent? You must always be consistent in how you apply all laws, rules, and policies. Where you can get into trouble is deviating from what the law actually says. If you are ever in doubt, seek professional guidance from a school lawyer or other administrative personnel. Laws, rules, and policies were developed for the purpose of creating fair and equitable conditions, so rely on them for direction.

Principals must have the ability to be impartial; not to show favorites with students, teachers, or anyone else; to be sensitive to student race, gender, language, learning, and religion, as well as other issues in interactions with all people. How you act and behave will tell more about what you value than what you actually say. Be sure to seriously reflect on these issues to be sure your heart is pure because, believe me, if it isn't, it will show sooner or later. Issues of integrity, fairness, and ethics should be topics of regular discussion and interaction with your Induction Partnership team.

Act Ethically

Many states and professional organizations have their own codes of ethics for professional behaviors. I require my graduate students to read and respond to the Code of Ethics and Professional Practices for Texas Educators (http://www.sos.state.tx.us/). Many of them voice surprise that tenets so basic to human behavior and good manners would need to be organized into a Code of Ethics. Someone always points out that if some people didn't act inappropriately, there would be no need for a Code of Ethics. Unfortunately, we do have people that act inappropriately so we do have a Code of Ethics.

Making the right decision can still be difficult sometimes because not all issues are cut and dried. In some instances there are good and bad outcomes to any decision you might make. In these times, there is absolutely nothing wrong with asking other administrators whom you respect what they would do in a similar circumstance. That doesn't mean you will actually do what they suggest, but at least you can get an outside perspective. Meetings with your Induction Partnership team are also a perfect venue for discussing ethical issues. People in that group care about your success. They will provide a sounding board, ask you reflective questions, and seek to offer guidance to help you make the right decision. Remember the West Point Cadet Prayer (Box 7.1) that we discussed earlier. Sometimes it is a lot easier to take the easy way out by making a wrong but popular decision instead of the right but more difficult decision. As long as you can explain your decisions based on ethical and legal principles, you can hold your head high knowing you made the right choice, even though it was difficult. In the end, that is what all of life is all about.

PROBLEM-BASED LEARNING

The School Built of Straw

When Dan Hopkins was selected as the new principal of Pedernales Elementary School, he was excited to receive the promotion from his former position as an assistant in another district. Pedernales had a good reputation, and Dan was happy to have the opportunity to put some of his ideas into practice. The school had been without a permanent principal for quite some time and was hungry for direction and leadership. It would seem like an ideal situation for a new principal. Dan would be coming to an established school with a good reputation that had faculty and staff who were eager for a new principal to provide leadership. Unfortunately, things are rarely what they seem to be from the outside.

For internal district reasons, the selection process had been long and drawn out. Finally, a procedure was established and the position posted. Voices of various school, district, and community members were solicited. Diverse faculty and staff members were elected by their peers to serve on the selection committee. The superintendent appointed additional members from other schools and the community. He also chose a central office administrator to serve as chair. The chair would provide the voice of the committee to him. He met with the committee once, gave them his charge, and then they were on their own.

Although there were multiple stakeholders involved, the selection process was not without its problems. The superintendent's appointment of the chair and additional members without election raised serious trust issues within the faculty regarding his intent and the efficacy of the upcoming selection process. Did he have an "agenda" for their school? Did he think they were incapable of selecting appropriate community members who had a sincere interest in their school? They felt concerned, degraded, and unappreciated by these appointments. The superintendent felt that adding the additional members would add balance and perspective, but faculty members felt they had been selected simply to report directly back to him about who was saying what and which applicants were being considering. They perceived a general lack of faith on his part that they were competent to make a credible recommendation for their new principal. They were also seriously concerned that they did not get to elect their chair, especially because the person he selected was someone who worked directly for him. Had he already selected someone he wanted as principal and then "stacked the deck" with his appointees to guarantee that person would be selected?

As the selection process developed, Dan was chosen almost by default. Because of the shortage of quality candidates in the applicant pool, Dan was the "lesser of the evils." The superintendent knew him from various community activities and readily approved the choice. Although most of the faculty members were willing to give Dan the benefit of the doubt, others felt he was selected to be the superintendent's yes-man. They were concerned about whether he would consistently have the best interests of the school and students in mind or would instead do whatever the superintendent told him to do, regardless of its impact on teaching and learning.

At the time of Dan's arrival, the school was undergoing a series of major programmatic and curricular changes; additional transitions were required by No Child Left Behind and state regulations. During this time, Dan sometimes appeared overwhelmed by the details of the task, but he went forward gallantly. His interest seemed somewhat divided between taking care of business at the school and spending what some considered unreasonable amounts of frivolous time with the superintendent, other central office administrators, and community leaders. From Dan's perspective, he was building necessary allegiances within the school community to better serve the school. From the faculty's perspective, he was merely absent. Still, during his initial induction period he was considered a bright, friendly fellow who was a forward thinker, even if he wasn't always around.

As time progressed, faculty began to sense a decline in his opinions about certain programs and people. More members of the school community began to lose faith in his commitment, thinking the time he spent away from school was a tool to advance his career at their expense. As Dan's networking for his individual job and professional future stability grew, his personal credibility at school diminished. His visibility with students was negligible, he avoided any meetings with parents, and his interpersonal skills working with faculty became curt and sometimes degrading. Students barely knew who he was. Worse, he began to belittle school culture, heroes, and heroines as if they were beneath him. He developed a condescending and cynical attitude that caused faculty to avoid him if at all possible. He had a bad habit of having faculty favorites, but the favorites changed frequently and for no apparent reason. A teacher or program that was in the spotlight might be discredited without warning. Teachers and students were constantly treated inconsistently, according to his "mood of the day." He seemed insecure or jealous of other people's successes. Instead of celebrating them, he either ignored or downplayed them. Not wanting to fall into that trap, formerly innovative faculty and staff quit doing anything creative. Their goal was to fade into the woodwork so as not to catch his attention or wrath. The culture of the school changed from being warm and student centered to isolated, disconcerted, fragmented, and off balance.

As the situation at Pedernales worsened, Dan was either oblivious or did not care. As long as he had the superintendent's support, school morale seemed irrelevant to him. Faculty members became increasingly concerned about his mood swings and were afraid to approach him. What he said one day may not be true the next. There was frequent concern that various people and programs were being set up or sabotaged. Dan's reactions and responses to people and things were arbitrary and had no apparent ethical standards. As the faculty members drew closer together in an attempt at self-protection, Dan continued to expand on his newfound friendships with the central office and community. Although there was now an official principal, Pedernales was, in truth, still a leaderless school—and a pretty pitiful one at that. Faculty fervently wished for the good old days when their interim principal involved them in decision making and valued their input. From the outside, Pedernales looked like a great school with a strong forward-thinking principal. From the inside, it was a school built of straw. Faculty waited and watched for the wind that would blow it away, hoping none of them or the students would be further hurt in the collapse.

REFLECTIVE ANALYSIS

Act With Integrity

1. Compare and contrast the issues of integrity, fairness, and ethics. What do they have in common? In what ways do they differ?

2. Many faculty members saw Dan as the poster boy for lack of integrity and scruples. Obviously, Dan is either not aware or does not care that his actions are perceived in this manner. Describe a nonconfrontational plan for Dan's Induction Partnership team to bring him back in touch with reality.

3. After meeting with his Induction Partnership team, Dan becomes defiant. He asserts that people are taking his behaviors out of context or distorting them. He is upset that his team has so little faith in him. How should the team respond?

4. After considerable time and tact, Dan finally accepts that maybe he has something to do with the problems at Pedernales. He seems ready to make efforts to reassess his behaviors and attitudes. Can this relationship be saved? Why or why not? If so, what can be done?

5. In working with Dan, he references problems in his personal life but does not detail them. There is a fine line between an administrator's personal life and his or her professional behavior. Should the Induction Partnership team touch this subject or leave it alone? Why or why not?

Act Fairly

1. Appraise Dan's situation and recreate it to solve his various problems in a fair and equitable manner.

2. The faculty and staff at Pedernales have lost trust and respect for Dan because he treats people in ways they perceive as unfair. Respect and trust are easy to lose and hard to regain. Can they be regained in this situation? If so, describe things Dan will have to do to regain them.

3. Part of the problem Dan experienced at Pedernales was the lack of a clearly articulated vision for the school. In what ways could this problem have been addressed before it got out of hand?

4. Sometimes these same issues are problems with experienced principals who have been left to their own devices without accountability for their actions. Part of the role of the Induction Partnership Model is to facilitate growth within each team member. Brainstorm a situation in which a team member other than the inductee is the one having ethical problems. How can the team be helpful in a supportive manner?

5. Role-play potential scenarios in which members of the Induction Partnership team address issues of integrity, ethics, and fairness with any new principal.

Act Ethically

1. After analyzing Dan's behavior patterns, prioritize the top three issues that must be addressed.

2. Formulate a plan that addresses these areas with goals, strategies, and assessment for Dan to grow personally and ethically.

3. If Dan does not make a genuine effort to change his ways and reestablish a good organizational culture, climate, and morale at his school, should he be removed as administrator? Why or why not?

4. What potential legal issues would have to be addressed to remove Dan from his position?

5. Create your own individual code of ethics, addressing integrity, fairness, and personal accountability to treat all people and issues with dignity, honor, and respect.

APPLICATION OF THE INDUCTION PARTNERSHIP MODEL

1. Looking at the first six Educational Leadership Constituent Council standards, identify three goals per standard to help Dan develop and grow as an administrator for Pedernales Elementary School.

2. How could the Induction Partnership Model be applied at Pedernales to help Dan succeed? Elaborate on the basic model to create an individualized growth plan for him. Include specific ways that the team could help Dan realize his weaknesses. What can be done to help him develop in the areas integrity, fairness, and ethics without causing him to react with a defensive, combative, or passive-aggressive attitude?

3. Identify and elaborate on strategies that each of the following stakeholders could utilize to help Dan meet his goals for integrity, fairness, and ethics:

   • Self (in this case, Dan)
   • Mentor

- District
- University or certifying agency
- Business and school community partnerships
- Family and friends

4. What resources will be needed for each participant to fulfill his or her responsibilities? Utilizing all stakeholders, how could these resources best be solicited and utilized?

5. Develop accountability measures for each goal to ensure that growth and measurement are occurring as planned and in a proactive and timely manner. Determine as a team how these issues can be brought before the group on a continuing basis to ensure development is taking place.

6. Design an ideal application of the Induction Partnership Model to help you grow in your current situation with regard to integrity, fairness, and ethics.

CONCLUSIONS

Being an administrator is a difficult job. You will be faced with decisions to make on things you never would have dreamed could come up. But they will come up, and they won't go away. You will have to take a stand. Even if people do not agree with your choice, if they know you truly listened, reflected, and cared about what was going on rather than just blowing it off, it can make an unwanted decision much easier to bear. Always remember that no one cares how much you know until they know how much you care. Show concern. Don't be afraid of appearing weak because you let your heart show. Our world already has way too many cynics! We could use a lot more concern, compassion, and empathy. Continuously look inside yourself to reflect on what your personal values are, who you are, and who you want to be. These are things all of us should be doing on a regular basis. To quote Fleetwood Mac, "Don't stop thinking about tomorrow." We live for another day, and life goes on.

When you are struggling over making the right decisions, remember Helen Keller. She faced so much adversity in her life. Who could be better to give us proper perspective on our role in life when we are feeling defeated, worthless, or insignificant in doing what is right as an advocate for all students? She appears to have been influenced by an inspirational minister, Edward Everett Hale, for she paraphrased one of his prayers often in her lifetime. Helen Keller had a dramatic impact on our world. So can you.

I am only one,
But still I am one.
I cannot do everything,
But still I can do something;
And because I cannot do everything
I will not refuse to do the something that I can do.

—Edward Everett Hale

ACTIVITIES FOR ADMINISTRATOR INDUCTION AND PROFESSIONAL DEVELOPMENT

The Standards-Based "Sweet 16" Induction Developmental Activities

- Consult with administrators on proper ways to handle inappropriate teacher or staff behavior in a manner that exhibits integrity, fairness, and ethics.
- Observe and analyze other administrators' methods of handling difficult students and parents that exhibit integrity, fairness, and ethics.
- Demonstrate impartiality to students, teachers, and families. Never show favorites.
- Develop a conflict-resolution plan that incorporates morality and integrity issues in working with families and community members.
- Develop and implement a plan to conduct frequent informal "walk-through" observations to show support for ongoing professional work that focuses on positive instead of negative behaviors that are observed.
- Facilitate the development and implementation of a school discipline committee with teachers to develop and support successful classroom management strategies.
- Organize an interactive creative session on ethics as part of the beginning of the school training for all staff members.
- Ensure that all federal, state, and local laws, as well as school board policies, are being consistently and appropriately followed.
- Demonstrate integrity and fairness in all situations.
- Set a standard of high expectations by consistently praising teachers and others on the good things that are happening.
- Base decisions on empirical data rather than on hunches, perceptions, or gossip.

- Provide diversity training to ensure faculty and staff understanding and appreciation of cultural, gender, racial, learning, and socio-economic differences.
- Personally reflect and seek input from others to see if there is anything you do that other might consider unethical.
- Respect and protect confidentiality laws.
- Initiate ethical role-playing opportunities for faculty and staff to practice potentially volatile interactions in dealing with students, parents, or others.
- Consistently document communications between staff and faculty members, parents, and others in the learning community.

8 Mama Told Me There'd Be Days Like This

Nothing will ever be attempted, if all possible objections must first be overcome.

—Samuel Johnson

STANDARD 6

Candidates who complete the program are educational leaders who have the knowledge and ability to promote the success of all students by understanding, responding to, and influencing the larger political, social, economic, legal, and cultural context.

TOP TEN THINGS ADMINISTRATORS WISH THEY HAD KNOWN BEFORE ENTERING THE PRINCIPALSHIP

Principals must

1. Never be dictators when dealing with stakeholders (parents, faculty, staff, students, etc.).

2. Learn how to cooperate when facilitating school improvement.

3. Empower others to be successful by sharing the work, responsibilities, and rewards.

4. Never act out of anger in regard to student disciplinary or other issues. Principals take the time they need to calm down and reflect to be able to make a prudent decision.

5. Be aware that all decisions are not cut and dried.

6. Understand, implement, and monitor school spending and the budgetary process.

7. Comprehend and implement all legal requirements of the educational system, including due process procedures and child custody issues.

8. Analyze and ensure that the numerous local, state, and federal reports that are their responsibility are done correctly and on time.

9. Understand, influence, and respond to all political facets of organizational oversight including personnel issues, district policies, curriculum changes, the budgetary process including Title I, state compensatory, and local funding, English as a Second Language (ESL) requirements and procedures, scheduling, discipline, and testing.

10. Never lose their sense of humor. Even the crankiest parent, student, faculty, or staff member likes to laugh. Using appropriate sensitivity, attempt to diffuse volatile situations.

PHILOSOPHICAL FRAMEWORK

The honored evangelist Billy Graham was being chauffeured to an event when he asked his driver to pull over. "I'm bored," he said. "Let's switch places. Let me drive for a while!" The driver didn't know quite what to make of this, but he did as instructed and changed places with Billy.

Being an older gentleman, Billy wasn't used to the high-powered engine in this particular car. He got a little "foot heavy" and, wouldn't you know it, the cops pulled him over for speeding!

When the policeman asked to see his driver's license Billy sheepishly gave it to him. The policeman looked at the name and picture, then looked at Billy, and then looked back at the picture. At that point, he went back to his squad car and radioed his captain.

"Sir, you are not going to believe who I just pulled over," he said.

"Who?" asked his boss.

"It's somebody really big," the policeman said with awe in his voice. They went back and forth several times with the captain wondering if it was the mayor, the governor, and various sports figures. Each time the policeman kept saying, "No, it's somebody bigger than that."

Finally, in sheer desperation, the captain asked, "Well, who is it?"

"Well, I'm not sure, sir, but his driver is Billy Graham so I'm guessing it must be God."

Of course, this story really didn't happen. Billy Graham did not get foot-heavy in a limousine or get pulled over for speeding. Yet for school administrators today, it is just about as easy to draw a wrong conclusion as the policeman did. Judgment, analysis, communication, and political skills are so important to school leaders. Issues that should not be a big deal have a way of turning into really big problems before you know it. Then there are times when you think something is going to turn into a disaster and nothing comes of it. It is so difficult to tell. For these reasons, being able to understand, respond to, and influence the larger context in which decisions are made can be the difference between success and failure for both new and experienced principals.

This is not the visionary leadership as described in Standard 1 or the nuts and bolts leadership of Standard 3. Somewhere in between must come the intuitive insights necessary to make astute decisions and resolve conflicts that impact immediate issues as well as the larger political, social, economic, legal, and cultural contexts of schools and learning. When it comes right down to it, exactly what kind of decisions could possibly be made that would not impact any of these factors? None. Therefore, the ability to make savvy political judgments can be the skill that either makes or breaks a new principal. Remember, as Mother Teresa said, we must believe in the power of one single person as a change agent to make a difference in schools and society. That person must be us, even when the decisions are hard.

Understand the Larger Context

The larger context of a situation is the influence that choices and actions can have on the greater school and community in addition to the immediate situation. For example, granting permission for the eighth-grade dance to be held on the evening of the same day that major standardized testing is occurring could distract students from the tests. Even though there are no conflicts on the calendar for that specific night, in the total picture, having a dance during major standardized testing may not be in the best interests of scores. Therefore, it is important for principals to always be looking ahead in a proactive manner, beginning with the end in mind, and playing their own devil's advocate to every situation. Sometimes the smallest of decisions can have a way of snowballing and coming back to haunt you simply because you did not think the whole thing through.

As principals and other administrators gain experience and perspective, this will become easier, but it will always be important. This is why it's a definite asset to have an Induction Partnership team to bounce ideas off of and who will help ask probing contextual questions you may not have thought about. You also must be able to research anything that could have a long-range effect on your decision.

To do this you must be aware of the legal and political systems in place to understand the inner nuances of how they work so you can respond appropriately. Sometimes you may feel there are laws, rules, or economic factors that are inappropriate for the best interests of students or families. But they are still the law. We don't have to love them, but we do have to follow them. Do not feel distraught or discouraged, and don't give up. There is hope! All you have to do is work your tail off as an activist to get those laws or rules changed. Do not say this is impossible or unrealistic. After all, someone has to be an advocate for the needs of every student, including those living in poverty or with other disadvantages. What you want to do is to get other people, families, community members, teachers, and others to help. Become actively involved in professional organizations that support educational causes, and make the most of technology as you search Web sites for appropriate resources to support the causes of children (see Table 8.1). Use the team approach we have discussed to involve multiple people from diverse factions of the community, then develop, articulate, and implement your plan to change anything that gets in the way of doing what is most appropriate to meet the needs of every student.

You might be thinking, "Good grief! I'm a principal, not a lobbyist!" Well, you may not be a paid lobbyist, but you are working for and representing the grassroots of society and the most oppressed and under-represented: our children. And our children are our future. Remember our For the Future party from Chapter 6? Well, here it is again. Go get a few recruits. You know what the U.S. Marines say: "All we need is a few good men." We are much broader in our approach. All we want are about a zillion good men *and women* so we can effectively make the world a better place for children. To do that we must address change and improvement from the most basic of American institutions: our schools. We are the leaders of these schools. So, yes, we must be the activists and advocates necessary to see to it that the best of opportunities are available for everyone.

The effects of the economy and poverty on student learning have long been documented. Children from homes with scarcities of resources often have fewer exposures to literacy and other constructivist activities

Table 8.1   Web Sites of Major Professional Associations and Organizations

Organization	Web Link
American Association of School Administrators	http://www.aasa.org
American Association of School Personnel Administrators	http://www.aaspa.org
American Educational Research Association	http://www.aera.net
Association of Supervision and Curriculum Development	http://www.ascd.org
Council of Chief State School Officers	http://www.ccso.org
Educational Leadership Constituent Council	http://www.npbea.org/elcc
National Association of Elementary School Principals	http://www.nasesp.org
National Association of School Boards	http://www.nasb.org
National Association of Secondary School Principals	http://www.nassp.org
National Council for Professors of Educational Administration	http://www.ncpea.net
National Council for the Accreditation of Teacher Education	http://www.ncate.org
National Middle School Association	http://www.nmsa.org
University Council for Educational Administration	http://www.ucea.org
United States Department of Education, Office of Elementary and Secondary Education	http://www.ed.gov/offices/OSES

that broaden the language and learning experiences necessary for academic success. The causes of poverty have long been debated and will not be resolved here, but there is one thing we know for sure: Although there are exceptions, there is also a long history of a cycle of poverty. Children raised poor are likely to remain poor, while children raised in middle- and upper-class environments are likely to be successful. So if your Induction Partnership Team suggests that you begin studying the business section of your newspaper, listening to CNN, or subscribing to the *Wall Street Journal*, they are advising it for more reasons than improving your stock portfolio. They are suggesting it because of the direct impact of the economy on families living in poverty and their children's success in school.

Our role is to help break the cycle of poverty. Sure, we know many people have been working on this for years. The fact that this cycle of poverty still exists is not a reason to quit trying to change it. We must delve into the effects of poverty and other disadvantages students face and their effects on schools and learning. You might wonder: If the U.S. Department of Education has put vast research dollars into questions such as these and not come up with standard answers, how could you? The answer is that the federal government is not actively engaged in knowing the needs, concerns, and situational contexts that exist in your school community. But you do. Having implemented Standard 4 on collaborative partnerships, you are already working with a team of diverse people who know well the contexts of all these factors in their neighborhoods. These "grassroots" people now become your experts. Together you should spend time talking about the causal agents behind these situations, what can be done to address them, and how this can relate specifically to improved student learning at your school. We talk, talk, and talk. Everything is about talking and communicating until together, ideas are initiated that result in plans that will make a difference for now and the future once implemented.

As we know, there are multiple diverse factors that affect schools and learning. The cultural diversity of most schools today is increasing. There are teachers who are not prepared to deal with the changing needs of these students and the consequences of their presence in classrooms on the way they teach. These teachers need the appropriate training to help them "retool" to understand, appreciate, and respond to these needs.

Those teachers are not the ones you need to worry about. You provide them the guidance they need, and they will be successful. The ones to worry about are those who don't want to change. They want the world to go back to "the good old days." Not only are they still looking for Beaver Cleaver's class, they want to teach it! To their great chagrin, they're not finding it. It is not the job of students to change the way they learn. It is the job of teachers to change the way they teach so as to teach students in the most appropriate and effective way possible. If most of the students are "failing," it is not their fault. It is the fault of poor instructional strategies and curriculum that does not relate to their needs. If teaching is done on their level and meets their needs, they will learn. As educators, we must study trends in demographic changes and rethink how we will address these changes. No child should be left behind. Every child is guaranteed a free and *appropriate* public education. It is our job to see that they get it by seeking to understand and respond to community and cultural norms and values. Connecting these norms and values with maximized and relevant educational opportunities are our first steps toward social justice in our society and nation.

Obviously, if you come into a new school situation and are foaming at the mouth about all the changes that must be made, the immediate reaction of the faculty and staff will be to run you out of town. This is not going to solve anything. So you must be patient, work together with the school to develop a vision that addresses the needs of all students, and work from there outward. The vision may not be all you wished it could be in the beginning. But babies learn to crawl before they learn to walk. In fact, research has shown that babies that skip crawling end up with certain developmental handicaps in later life. Too much change up front can create problems that are counterproductive to the ultimate goals of social justice. You must be patient and take things step by step by step. Stick with the plan.

Regardless of how you lead, there will always be conflict of various kinds. A certain amount of conflict is healthy because it means there is a diversity of ideas rather than "Smallville Goes to School" whereby everyone has the exact same homogeneous belief system. When conflict gets out of hand, tempers flare, and people begin to get hurt, there is too much conflict; discussions have crossed the line from a healthy exchange of ideas to negativity. Your skills at diplomacy, problem solving, conflict resolution, and consensus building are critical to the long-term health and productivity of the school and community as well as your survival. This is another target point for you to address with your Induction Partnership team members as you seek guidance from their expertise and experience in potential volatile situation. The basic idea is to never let conflict go that far, to nip it in the bud by defusing it. The harder question is how to defuse it while still holding onto the culture and collegiality of the group. The main step is to always keep refocusing everyone on what is best for students rather than what is popular or easier. We learned long ago from King Arthur that often "might" is not "right." We know from the West Point Cadet Prayer (see Box 7.1) that doing what is right is often more difficult than giving up and allowing things to happen that are not right. It will take courage, strength, and fortitude for you to do what needs to be done. But you can do it. Just hold on to your base understanding of the core values, interests, and needs of your school and community; understand the larger implications of everything that is said or done; and be ready to face the challenges that continue to come your way. In doing these things consistently, you will develop the trust and loyalty of your faculty, staff, students, their families, and the community. As long as you have your integrity, you and your school will rise to the top.

Respond to the Larger Context

Throughout this book, and particularly in Chapters 3 and 6, we have placed great emphasis in developing relationships and partnerships with all sorts of people and groups inside and outside the school. The development of relationships could easily be the most critical thing for a new principal to learn and cultivate. For some people doing this does not come naturally and can only be achieved through great effort. For others, cultivating people isn't difficult at all. It is part of their innate personality.

Regardless of which group you fall into, these relationships are critical to your success in being able to know, understand, and *respond* to the larger context of schools and communities.

Interactions are built around communication. The combination of the verbal and nonverbal ways you communicate say a lot about you and your leadership style. Two people can say the exact same thing with different nuances and body language and convey radically different messages. Take, for example, the simple phrase, "Oh, really?" It can be said sarcastically with rolling eyes and crossed arms. Or it can be said with sensitivity, direct eye contact, and loose arms. The messages sent and received are totally different. To be effective leaders, we must also send a message of caring. Consider an old adage: "No one cares how much you know until they know how much you care." Active listening, eye contact, and interpersonal sensitivity, rather than interruptions and insistent tones, can make all the difference in the world.

Active listening and communicating doesn't just happen for those who are uncomfortable with new people and situations. These skills must be practiced with conscientious effort, but you will use them constantly when working with people who like you as well as with those who don't. It is especially important, but also especially difficult, to practice patience and understanding with people whose goal you believe is to sabotage you. Sometimes it comes as a shock to new principals that everyone doesn't come to the school with the purest of hearts. There really are some people who simply like to cause trouble. Sometimes their favorite thing is to make trouble for *you*. It makes their day.

In those instances you may want to tell them what you really think of them and their crummy non-student-centered attitude, but you can't. You must respond to whatever their "concern" is, but you must do it politely. After they leave, you can scream and bang your head against the wall, but not until then. You must be a lady or a gentleman, but you do not have to take abuse. If they threaten you with physical force or profanity, ask them to leave, or leave yourself. If necessary, call security.

The most important point is to maintain ongoing conversations with people with different perspectives on many issues. Anything that helps the school succeed is worth doing and cultivating. We must remain cognizant of trends, issues, and potential changes in political, legal, cultural, economic, and all other areas that could impact teaching and learning.

Influence the Larger Context

Once we understand and take steps to respond to the larger context, we are at a point of attempting to *influence* societal factors. If there are laws, polices, or rules that are not in the best interest of students and schools, we will work with community members to facilitate their change. These regulations may be in regard to political, social, economic, legal, or cultural contexts as they concern students and educational issues. Activities should be planned to engage families and community members in actively improving anything that relates to school programs, policies, trends, and issues. The idea is to stay in contact with everyone all the time, continuously discussing and participating in ongoing assessment of anything that relates to schooling. We are back to the full red-alert status with which we started early in the book.

In summary, as school administrators it is our responsibility to address anything and everything that affects students and how they learn. Although it is impossible for you to do everything single-handedly, you must practice your skills at delegation and empowerment to let others participate in the things they can so you can focus your attention on things that will give education the most value. There will be times when you are tired and really do not want to speak up on controversial issues, but you will do it anyway because you know that you are the person others are looking to as the voice and face of the school. You are the educational leader, which includes the larger context of academics, physical, cultural, and psychological issues, trends, and development. You must be the advocate for equitable situations and opportunities for all students regardless of socioeconomics, ethnicity, gender, disability, or other individual characteristics. No one ever said school leadership was easy. Yes, we know there are principals in the field right now who do not do these things. But they are not you. You are the new breed of school leader who is an advocate for the individual needs of every child and who will run that race with ardor until your days are done.

PROBLEM-BASED LEARNING

Football Is King!

In many parts of the United States, football reigns as the king of high school sports. The lights shine bright on Friday nights as the band warms up, drill-teams high kick, cheerleaders yell, and concessions flow. The town shows up to watch those boys play ball. "Get 'em! Knock 'em dead! Score a touchdown . . . or two or three!" There are few things that can bring a town together quicker than a winning football team. Young and old alike enjoy the camaraderie, athletic prowess, civic unity, and plain old competitive spirit as the Tigers take on the Bulldogs and the Eagles whip the Bobcats.

There are also few things that communities like less then to lose week after week. "Why, it is just plain un-American! Fire that coach! Get us a new one! Get one that knows how to *win!*" Football fans may not remember the superintendent's name, but, by golly, they know who that losing football coach is, and they want him fired! Letters to the editor flow. Calls pour into radio talk shows. School board members have to disconnect their answering machines, and district administrators shake their heads in despair. "Why don't we have all this uproar over academics?" they wonder. Well, academics aren't playing East Chambers on Friday night, and the Trojans are!

That is exactly what took place at Ranch Valley High School, home of the Fighting Trojans. Ranch Valley is a medium-sized town with a population just under 70,000. They have a long history of good football teams and boast of several state championships. For the last five years, however, ever since "that Broderick guy" took over the team, a fairly decent record has gone from bad to worse. From seasons of 6–3 or better, they progressed to 4–5 to 4–4–1, and this year to 1–8. Game attendance was considerably down, and talks of the pitiful coach with no offense and no need for defense were the talk of every coffee shop and dry cleaner in town. Even the Rotarians shook their heads in despair. If the band weren't performing at halftime, what incentive would there have been for people to go to the games at all? Even with that, lots of folks left after the band marched. "At least we can win at halftime," the band parents said.

Belle Bagelman, principal at Ranch Valley High School, wondered how on earth she was supposed to focus on teaching and learning at the school when every former jock in town was calling her on the phone or showing up at her office demanding that ridiculous excuse of a coach be fired. Although Belle defended him as running a clean program and for placing a heavy emphasis on the athletes doing well in their classes, the Jock Club didn't care one little bit. All they could think of was another humiliating loss to East Chambers. And that simply would not do. "Fire that robot!" they cried. "Just get rid of him!"

Fortunately or unfortunately, Belle was not alone in her plight. Dr. Marable, the superintendent, was also receiving the same calls and visits. Worse, he was a member of the Rotary Club and got to hear it at breakfast as well. Then, if that weren't enough, the school board got tired of having their answering machines disconnected. They told Dr. Marable to "take care of the situation" so they wouldn't have to.

Realizing enough was enough, Dr. Marable and Belle got together to discuss the situation. Agreeing in principle that they had no desire to embarrass Coach Broderick beyond what he was all ready enduring, but also knowing things could not continue the way they were, they invited the coach to come visit with them about his future plans. In so doing, they learned he was just as miserable as they were. His phone was also ringing off the wall with ugly calls, he was getting almost-obscene anonymous letters in the mail, and his wife couldn't even go to the grocery store without feeling like people were staring at her and talking about her husband behind her back. Worse, it was probably true. Together, the three of them decided the coach would request reassignment to a full-time teaching position within the district.

Once this was announced, the Jock Club settled down, but only temporarily. It didn't take them any time at all to regroup with a new focus. "We want our favorite son to come home and coach the Trojans! He's a fine boy. We like him, and he knows how to win! Bring Johnny home!" New momentum mounted as the Have Johnny Come Marching Home Again Fan Club got rolling.

Just when school board members thought it was safe to answer the phone again, the Fan Club started calling. "When was the last time anything we did got this much attention?" they asked each other incredulously. No one could remember. It sure wasn't at public hearings regarding Title I or when they studied results of state-mandated tests.

Soon the position was posted, and candidates began to apply. Word went through the football grapevine like wildfire that Johnny was marching home again. People in the coaching community across the state heard it. Some potentially excellent candidates who were interested in the job did not apply because they thought Johnny had it wrapped up with a great big Trojan blue and silver bow. This upset both Belle and Dr. Marable, who both wanted an open and clean search for the new coach.

In the meantime, at the school board meeting the board appointed a committee consisting of the superintendent, personnel director, and high school principal to screen applicants after the deadline and bring them five finalists to interview. "What do you want us to do about Johnny?" Dr. Marable asked. "His Fan Club has the whole town riled up."

"Let's just see how it all works out after all the applications are in," the board members said as more applicants continued to come forward.

The committee worked hard to review the candidates and was pleased with many of their qualifications. The group was narrowed to four candidates with stellar credentials—plus Johnny. Although his record was good, it did not stack up to the rest of the finalists. But he was the local favorite son and the community members' perception was that he was the hero who would help them slaughter East Chambers next year. Belle, Dr. Marable, and the personnel director stared at each other in a quandary. "Now what do we do?" asked Belle.

"It's a puzzle," said the personnel director. "Johnny has good credentials, but not nearly as good as some of the others. Should we give in to community pressure and include him as a finalist or not?"

"The board is between a rock and a hard place," said Dr. Marable. "If we do not include Johnny as a finalist, they will catch heat from the community for not interviewing him. If we do, I don't see how they could give him the job based solely on his record. They'll still catch heat from the community. In fact, it could be worse than if he were not interviewed at all. They can't win."

"Yes, it's the community that really wants Johnny," said Belle. "The board really wants to hire the best coach and have this over with so we can move on to other things. Frankly, I'll be more than glad when it is over. We've got spring testing coming up. I need our teachers and parents to be focused on student performance, not next year's football team. What a year to have this happen! No Child Left Behind is in effect, yet here we are going on and on about who should coach the Trojans."

"The community had better be careful what they ask for," said the personnel director, "Or they just might get it."

"You're right," agreed Dr. Marable slowly.

"Go, Trojans," groaned Belle.

REFLECTIVE ANALYSIS

Understand the Larger Context

1. Identify and explain the nuances that go into making high school football such a compelling community activity.

2. In Ranch Valley, all students participating in extra- and co-curricular activities must pass every course to be eligible. Coach Broderick supports his athletes being strong students. Should this be considered as a job performance criterion for a coach? Why or why not?

3. Belle knows little about the intricacies of football; however, she is the high school principal. Should she have been a part of the coaching finalist selection committee? Why or why not?

4. Is it legal for Johnny to be selected as a finalist if there are other candidates with better records who are not selected? Support your response.

5. If Johnny is selected as head football coach and does not produce a winning team, what possible community ramifications might there be?

Respond to the Larger Context

1. Should the committee select Johnny as a finalist for the coaching position? Why or why not?

2. Define and discuss the role of the high school principal in working with the head coaches for all sports.

3. Define and discuss the role of the high school principal in working with the athletic director. What differences, if any, would apply if the athletic director's office was or was not at the school?

4. When job candidates actively engage the community in their support for a certain position, how should the principal respond to citizen pressure?

5. In what ways, if any, should the high school principal interact with athletic or other booster clubs that have fiscal accounts?

Influence the Larger Context

1. What influence should the principal exert in the selection of school personnel?

2. Should the school board give in to community pressure and hire Johnny, even though he is not the best candidate?

3. Develop a model for vertical alignment of elementary and secondary athletic programs to solicit community involvement in support of the district's mission.

4. In light of laws regarding freedom of speech, in what ways can administrators seek to get job candidates for any position to follow district application policies without overt incitement of community pressure for their hiring?

5. Describe and provide examples of the role of co- and extracurricular activities in supporting the school's vision and mission.

APPLICATION OF THE INDUCTION PARTNERSHIP MODEL

1. Looking at the first six Educational Leadership Constituent Council standards, identify three goals per standard to help Belle or Dr. Marable (or both) develop and grow as administrators targeting the political aspects of issues contained within each standard.

2. In what ways could the Induction Partnership Model be applied at Ranch Valley to help Belle or Dr. Marable succeed politically within the social, economic, legal, and cultural contexts of the community?

3. In what specific ways could Belle or Dr. Marable develop their skills in understanding, responding to, and influencing the larger political, social, economic, legal, and cultural contexts of school leadership?

4. Identify and elaborate on strategies that each of the following stakeholders could use to help Belle or Dr. Marable meet their goals for political, social, economic, legal, and cultural contexts in a collaborative manner:
   - Self (in this case, Belle or Dr. Marable)
   - Mentor
   - District
   - University or certifying agency
   - Business-school community partnerships
   - Family and friends

5. What resources will be needed for each participant to fulfill his or her responsibilities? Utilizing all stakeholders, how could these resources best be solicited and utilized?

6. Develop accountability measures for each goal to ensure that growth and assessment are occurring as planned and in a proactive and timely manner. Determine as a team how these issues can be brought before the group on a continuing basis to ensure development is taking place.

7. Design an ideal application of the Induction Partnership Model to help you grow in your current situation in regard to understanding, responding to, and influencing the larger political, social, economic, legal, and cultural contexts involved.

CONCLUSIONS

There is an old story of a man taking a walk on the beach at dusk. In the shadows ahead, he sees someone slowly and gracefully throwing starfish back out into the sea. Upon approaching, he asks the person why he is doing that. He responds that if left on the shore the starfish will die, so he is throwing them back out to the sea.

The walking man says, "That is ridiculous. There are thousands of starfish on the beach. You will never be able to make a difference for all of them. And even as you throw more starfish are being washed ashore. You are wasting your time."

Reaching down the thrower picks up another starfish and gracefully tosses it back out to sea. Then he turns to his greeter, slowly smiles, and says, "But I made a difference for that one."

How true! That is exactly the attitude we must have to understand, respond to, and influence the larger contexts and roles of schools in society. Sure, people have tried to change things in the past. Some have been successful. Others haven't. The fact that there are still poverty, inequities, and decisions made daily that are not in the best interests of students and learning are not reasons to give up. Instead they are only proof that we must continue to throw starfish back into the sea. We may not change the whole world, but we can at least make a difference for those around us.

ACTIVITIES FOR ADMINISTRATOR INDUCTION AND PROFESSIONAL DEVELOPMENT

The Standards-Based "Sweet 16" Induction Developmental Activities

- Identify community leaders and invite them to participate in school leadership and student development.
- Develop programs or activities that integrate the neighborhood's traditions and cultures into the school learning environment.
- Volunteer for districtwide and community committees as the voice and face of your school.
- Read and reflect on current research journals to be informed of best practices and changes in policies, politics, economics, social justice, and education.
- Establish an advisory team of diverse school and community stakeholders to discuss and make recommendations on issues that could affect the school's learning environment and productivity.
- Identify exemplary schools with similar demographic settings. Research factors that could be indicators of their success as well as how to modify and utilize them for success on your school.
- Dialogue and network with other administrators about their experiences to get other perspectives on how to address various issues appropriately.
- Attend professional workshops, meetings, seminars, and conferences to be well informed about legislative decisions and updates, particularly those regarding special education.

- Empower all stakeholders to ensure synergy and responsibility for the growth and prosperity of the school vision, culture, and climate.
- Facilitate collaborative and shared decision making among all stakeholders.
- Ensure teachers and staffs have effective and appropriate professional development in all areas including diversity and technology in a changing society.
- Know and understand the educational legal system and the ramifications of all decisions and behaviors.
- Facilitate the development and implementation of monthly support groups for families of special needs students.
- Attend city council and other community events to represent the school and to keep abreast of current political, cultural, and sociological interests and needs.
- Develop a collaborative working partnership with Child Protective Services and local police departments for the benefit of students, families, and others.
- Consistently facilitate others in being an advocate for all students in a free and democratic society.

9 The Internship

*Preservice Administrators
Looking to the Future*

You've got to find the force inside you.

—Joseph Campbell

STANDARD 7

The internship provides significant opportunities for candidates to synthesize and apply the knowledge and practice and develop the skills identified in Standards 1–6 through substantial, sustained, standards-based work in real settings, planned and guided cooperatively by the institution and school district personnel for graduate credit.

TOP TEN INDUCTION TIPS FOR INTERNS

1. Get a mentor and utilize the Induction Partnership Model!

2. Seek diverse internship activities and placements in more than one setting and neighborhood type to broaden your experiences and perspectives.

3. Solicit formative input and feedback from educators with diverse experiences and perspectives.

4. Never assume that you are dealing with people who have the same understanding of professional behavior that you do.

5. Don't make hasty decisions. Take time to think things through and analyze the situation. Don't say everything you are thinking.

6. Understand your time limitations and organize accordingly.

7. Know the character of the people surrounding you and determine who you can trust.

8. Don't let the job go to your head. Remember that we are all mere humans.

9. Understand that not everything is black and white. Seek multiple perspectives and the use of reliable data in decision making.

10. Don't sweat the small stuff, or the stress will kill you.

PROBLEM-BASED LEARNING

The University of Texas at Arlington

The University of Texas at Arlington (UTA) is located in the heart of the Dallas–Fort Worth metropolitan area. It is the second largest component of the vast University of Texas System. With an enrollment of approximately 24,000 students, the university is large, diverse, and urban. Long known for excellence in its programs of engineering, science, architecture, business, and nursing, UTA is a relative newcomer as an educator preparation entity, having only been certifying teachers since 1963. Originally founded within the Liberal Arts Department of Psychology, education became the stand-alone Center for Professional Teacher Education in 1978. Because of the intense growth and recognition of UTA teacher preparation programs and the addition of school administration programs in the principalship and superintendency, the center officially became the School of Education in 1999.

Prior to 1993, teachers could not receive master's degrees or certification in any form of school leadership at UTA. At the time of the Educational Leadership program's inception, developers led extensive forums to solicit Dallas–Fort Worth metroplex school, business, and industry input into the way the subsequent program(s) should be formed as well as the things students finishing the program should know and be able to perform in schools for increased PreK–12 student learning performance. These forums were held over the course of two years both on the UTA campus and in extensive school-based sites. These sites were geographically selected because of the extremely large and populous area that UTA primarily serves. In an effort to develop partnerships the forums were actually hosted by different school districts rather than the university. This produced greater buy-in from the districts as well as empowerment and autonomy for the school-centered programs that were being developed.

The highest priority of the districts and other metroplex stakeholders providing input was that a yearlong, preferably full-time, paid internship was critical to the recruitment, identification, and development of future school leaders. Using these insights, two initial programs were developed (Wilmore, 2000; Wilmore & Thomas, 1998). The first program was self-paced. Students move through this program independently, taking courses that were directly linked to state standards. They are not in a cohort.

The second program called Educational Leadership UTA was our original, totally field-based principal preparation program (Wilmore, 1999; Wilmore & McNeil, 1999). Originally designed to target underrepresented populations for leadership positions, it was the first and only program within the state to integrate public, private, charter, and for-profit schools successfully into one cohesive principal preparation program. Participating districts were given the autonomy to recruit and select interns for a one-year totally field-based administrative cohort program. Coursework was integrated throughout the year as professors worked together with multiple school, district, and community field experiences. Interns were placed at schools chosen by their districts, removed from their teaching positions for one year, and paid as full-time administrative interns. Upon completion of the program, students received a master's degree in educational administration, and upon successful passage of the Texas certification exam, they became certified as school administrators. More than 100 Educational Leadership UTA alumni are currently filling positions of responsibility on state, district, school, and community leadership levels. Many have gone on to pursue doctoral degrees.

Based on the success of Educational Leadership UTA, the Hurst-Euless-Bedford Independent School District (HEBISD) approached UTA about developing an additional field-based cohort specifically for their teachers. This program, called the Scholars of Practice, was originally implemented exclusively within the HEBISD through an extensive collaborative between the university and district. It was developed to address the unique needs of their district and the administrative retirement turnover they were facing in the next five years. Both university and school district personnel worked together to teach courses specifically designed to meet the changing needs and diversity of this district. Classes were actually taught in the school district instead of at the university because faculty made a commitment to make the program as accessible as possible. Although not completely released from their teaching positions, provisions are made within the district for extensive field experiences over an 18-month period. As with Educational Leadership UTA, university and district personnel mutually supervise and mentor interns. This program is so successful that it has now been replicated and additional cohorts opened to potential students from other school districts. A cohort now also meets at the UTA Riverbend campus located in Fort Worth.

Continuing to grow and expand while still desiring to collaborate and further meet the needs of metroplex districts, UTA now offers a variation of these cohort models within the Dallas Independent School District that expounds on the components of the Educational Leadership UTA program with an urban leadership focus. Also interesting about this cohort is that the Dallas ISD, UTA, and the University of Texas at Dallas partnered to sponsor it, forming a collaborative partnership between two universities and one of the nation's largest and most diverse school districts. This proves that a large, urban school district and more than one university can successfully partner to meet district and student needs and address the great shortage of appropriately trained urban school leaders. Students within the cohort may register for different course credits through each university, but their degree will come from the University of Texas at Arlington. The key is not to focus on barriers but to ask, "What can we do to make this work? What can we do to make it better? How can we create mutually beneficial situations of which the end product remains the same—improving PreK–12 student performance through better preparation of school leaders?"

In Texas, a difficult certification examination is required for all educators, including school administrators, completing preparation programs. All educator preparation entities, whether university based, alternative, or through education service centers, are evaluated based on student performance on these exams. Scores are tabulated by both race and gender. Students within each subgroup must meet state standards or their programs will be placed under strict state review. If scores are too poor, the university can lose its ability to certify educators. Therefore, student performance on these standards-based tests is essential both to student success and university accreditation. Texas, it seems, was a forerunner for certain No Child Left Behind mandates. Based in large part on the success of our collaboration and partnerships with so many districts and entities, UTA students yearly score high within all subgroups on the state certification examinations.

There are several specific points that have direct impact on the success of these UTA programs. Each program is directly aligned with Texas certification domains and competencies as well as the national Educational Leadership Constituent Council (ELCC) standards. The seventh ELCC standard on internships prescribes that programs be substantial, sustained, and standards based. The standard also prescribes that internships be placed in real settings, planned and guided cooperatively with school and university personnel working together, and that students obtain graduate credit for their work. Each of the UTA programs—both Scholars of Practice, the original Educational Leadership UTA cohort, and the new program, with its urban emphasis—meet these criteria.

Let's see how.

PHILOSOPHICAL FRAMEWORK

Internships That Are Substantial, Sustained, and Standards Based

Each University of Texas at Arlington program has received initial and ongoing policy-based assessment by internal and external evaluators to ensure quality delivery of substantial and sustained coursework. Each class in every program has a field composition, utilizes technology, and has an action research component of some kind that focuses on PreK–12 student learning and school improvement. In each program there is a specified matrix or layout to Texas and ELCC standards such that all students are assured of having every competency addressed in multiple settings. Each of these standards is addressed in a variety of ways through the connection of theory to practice. Students are required to complete numerous assignments, each of which is directly linked to state and national standards. In this manner, all students, regardless of program, are exposed and integrated into authentic standards-based activities that are based on research and best practice but that are also practical and relevant to contemporary school issues and improvement.

Internships in Real Settings, Planned and Guided Cooperatively, and for Graduate Credit

Details of the structure of each internship experience vary from program to program. However, each internship is in a real setting, is planned and guided cooperatively between university faculty and school personnel, and is worth two semesters of graduate credit. For example, interns in both Educational Leadership UTA cohorts do not teach at all. They serve as full-time, paid administrative interns for a one-year period. This is the best of all worlds, but not all schools can afford to pay an intern while they are in graduate school without them still occupying a teaching position. Students in the self-paced program and the Scholars of Practice program are in that situation. The distinction is, for any student to participate in any of our internship programs, their districts and identified mentor administrator(s) must sign and commit to collaboratively developed intern and mentor guidelines that are directly tied to the substantial, sustained, standards-based curriculum and experience. In addition, each of their internships takes place in real school settings. We do not allow summer internships except in rare instances. In those instances, to guarantee an authentic experience, the student must do the internship in a summer or year-round school with learners present.

Throughout each internship, school district and university personnel mutually supervise students. Student portfolios, artifacts, logs, reflections, research projects, and other assignments are all tied to state and national standards. In each instance, students receive a minimum of six graduate credits over the course of their programs. Students in the cohorts move through their programs together. Students in the self-paced program do not, but they are still required to take two three-hour internships over a yearlong period.

Faculty and administration within the School of Education at the University of Texas at Arlington are committed to an ever-changing process of self and program evaluation to keep our programs on the cutting edge of school improvement initiatives. Over the past eight years, we have received close to $1 million in direct external support through grants from the Texas Education Agency, Texas Principals Leadership Initiative, and the Sid Richardson Foundation of Fort Worth for innovative principal preparation and assessment. This amount of external in-kind support from schools and districts is immeasurable as districts commit funds for salaries, professional development, mentoring, and, in some cases, intern travel and graduate school tuition, books, and fees. This mutual commitment of funds between external grants, schools, districts, and the university manifests itself in graduates who are prepared to meet the changing roles of democratic school leaders today.

Access to such large sums of money is not mandatory, however, to creating, nurturing, and sustaining a substantial, sustained, and standards-based program with important components in the field. What is essential is the university's ongoing commitment to create collaborative partnerships with the schools they serve. University stakeholders must constantly be asked "How can we serve you better? How can we work together to improve everything we do? How can we consistently assess our programs and relationships such that we never grow stagnant or rest on the laurels of our past successes?" When ongoing communication and evaluation is taking place on a regular basis, good things will happen. But it cannot happen in a vacuum. Universities must be the ones to initiate the relationships, to prove they want to be of true value, and that they are not so lodged in their "ivory towers" that they can't see the reality of the forest for the ideal of the trees. Necessity begets creativity and creativity is the brainchild of doing great things without extensive resources. To those who truly want to create lasting change and improvement, necessity becomes the mother of invention.

REFLECTIVE ANALYSIS

Internships That Are Substantial, Sustained, and Standards Based

1. Define and describe things that would make an ideal substantial internship. What components or special features would it have?

2. Define and describe things that would make an ideal sustained internship. What components or special features would it have?

3. Describe what is meant by a standards-based internship and a process to develop one.

4. Compare and contrast the internship you experienced with an ideal substantial, sustained, standards-based experience. In what ways would they be the same, different, or improved?

5. Explore obstacles to putting substantial, sustained, standards-based internships into place as well as potential solutions for universities, districts, or other certifying agencies to create collaboratively.

Internships in Real Settings, Planned and Guided Cooperatively, and for Graduate Credit

1. Define and elaborate on "real settings." What does this mean? What kind of setting is not real? How can these settings be made better?

2. For logistical and employment reasons too many administrative students do not have authentic, full-time internships. Identify reasons this occurs and potential creative solutions that the relevant entities (districts, schools, universities, other certifying agencies, etc.) could achieve based on these standards.

3. Some administrative interns continue to teach during the day and work to accumulate their internship clock hours and experiences

during their conference periods, before and after school. Analyze factors that contribute to this, pros and cons of its implementation, and ways to enhance the situation.

4. A common problem in administrative internships is that student experiences are not planned and guided cooperatively between the student, university, and school. Instead, interns are too often left to their own creativity to develop ways to document hours and experiences. Frequently their mentors readily agree to "sign off" on any university paperwork because they feel they do not have the time to sit down, guide, reflect, and truly mentor the student. Because of time constraints, university representatives commonly make quick school trips to see their intern and the mentor, but the trips often lack substance, focus, and depth. How could the Induction Partnership Model benefit this scenario?

5. In small groups, brainstorm ideas that would create a perfect learning situation for any student going through an administrative internship experience. Involve roles and responsibilities for the intern, their family, the mentor, university, district, and any others your group sees as developmentally important. Upon completion, present and discuss your model with others. Compare and contrast responses as well as what has been learned.

APPLICATION OF THE INDUCTION PARTNERSHIP MODEL

1. Looking at the first six Educational Leadership Constituent Council standards, identify three goals per standard to help future administrators develop, grow, and have authentic internship experiences. If you are a student or intern, identify three goals per standard of things you wish you knew more about and could have experiences with during your internship or induction year.

2. In what ways could the Induction Partnership Model be applied for future administrators experiencing their internships? In what specific manner could interns be helped to identify and expand on developmental activities addressing each of the initial six ELCC standards?

3. Identify and elaborate on strategies each of the following stakeholders could use to help interns meet their internship goals:

- Intern
- Mentor

- District
- University or certifying agency
- Business-school community partnerships
- Family and friends

4. What resources will be needed for participants to fulfill their responsibilities?

5. With the collaboration of all stakeholders, how could these resources best be solicited and utilized to improve the internship and induction periods for current and future administrators?

6. Develop accountability measures and a timeline for each goal to ensure that growth and assessment are occurring in a proactive and timely manner. Determine as a team how these issues can be brought before the group on a continuing basis to ensure that development is taking place.

7. Design an ideal application of the Induction Partnership Model to help you grow in your current situation by mentoring a current or future intern or new administrator that would subsequently enhance performance for each stakeholder, including yourself.

CONCLUSIONS

For future administrators to have authentic and substantive preparatory experiences, their internship must be more than clocking hours, wiping tables, checking in books, and doing cafeteria or bus duty or other routine school activities that require little thought and certainly not a master's degree. In all skilled professions, everyone—carpenters and plumbers, doctors and artists, musicians and lifeguards—must have the opportunity to practice and refine their capabilities. The same is definitely true for teachers and administrators. No reasonable person expects resident or intern physicians to practice and refine their skills in a random, haphazard manner; the same must be true for administrative interns. They, our schools, and our country deserve nothing less that a cooperatively designed and implemented plan of action for our future school leaders. Their experiences should not be random, but well thought out, built around state or national standards such as those of the ELCC, taking place in a real school with real students and faculty present and for graduate credit. They should receive recognition for the hard work they are doing. Further, their leadership development should be continuously monitored, assessed, and supported. Their daily activities must be consistently tailored to meet their individual needs as well as those of the school they are serving. Anything less is not good enough.

To continue leaving future school leaders floundering through lackadaisical internships that are not tied to standards or expectations is a shame, and this practice must stop immediately. Although not every internship can be full time, they can be planned and implemented through a joint partnership of university and school personnel. The Induction Partnership Model is the perfect framework to achieve this goal. It differentiates the roles and responsibilities of each team member, creates a timeline for implementation and assessment, and provides supportive yet corrective feedback from each participant. It is a model to turn "catch me if you can" hours into a cohesive framework built on research, best practice, cooperation, logic, and plain common sense. If it takes a village to raise a child, it takes the Induction Partnership Model to nurture, develop, and support a principal.

Good-bye, old-time internships! We're off to change administrator induction, one principal at a time!

ACTIVITIES FOR ADMINISTRATOR INDUCTION AND PROFESSIONAL DEVELOPMENT

The Standards-Based "Sweet 16" Induction Developmental Activities

- Study the different leadership styles of various administrators to see how they interact with other people, make decisions, involve others, and so on. Analyze which behaviors garner the best results and reflect on why this is the case.
- Make appointments to conference with several administrators who have diverse leadership styles and at different types of schools to observe the way they handle various circumstances. Explain their rationale.
- Spend time observing and talking with faculty, staff, and resource personnel that work with students of varying learning styles and abilities to learn how to best meet student needs.
- Study every facet of special education laws and regulations. Talk to as many teachers, counselors, diagnosticians, and others who have expertise and who work in these areas. You can never learn too much about special education.
- Attend school board meetings to understand the "big picture" of what is going on among administrators and the board. This will express your interest in the district and its leadership.

- Read, analyze, and reflect on research and best practice from various contemporary publications and other sources including those of professional organizations, major newspapers, and the Internet.
- Attend seminars, workshops, and classes on current trends in law, diversity, technology, and other issues to improve teaching and learning.
- Facilitate the establishment of an advisory team made up of community members, stakeholders, and teachers to discuss issues that could affect the school learning environment.
- Stay up-to-date on federal, state, and professional organization standards that affect teaching, learning, and leadership.
- Develop a current personal and professional library. Provide reading and resource recommendations to others based on individual interests and needs.
- Assist the school community through effective learning opportunities on multicultural and socioeconomic issues.
- Interview experienced school administrators and district business office personnel to assist the development of your knowledge and skills related to public school finance, budget planning, and management of resources.
- Analyze and understand your district and school policies and regulations on all issues.
- Participate in admission, review, and dismissal committee meetings to further understand how and why laws were developed to protect the rights of students to a free and appropriate public education.
- Assist in the development, implementation, and assessment of crisis management plans.
- Seek guidance and feedback from your mentor and other administrators as you actively practice collaborative and participatory leadership.

10 *For the Future*

It is far better to dare mighty things, to win glorious triumphs, even though checkered by failure, than to take rank with those poor spirits who neither enjoy much nor suffer much, because they live in the grey twilight that knows not victory nor defeat.

—Theodore Roosevelt

TOP TEN ALL-AROUND TIPS FOR NEW ADMINISTRATORS

1. Above all else, have a heart. Don't lose focus on why you became an administrator in the first place.

2. Remember that you are the school instructional leader. Try to keep everything else in perspective.

3. Even though you are busy, be sure that you continue to grow and learn, on both a personal and an academic level. Remember that to maximize your productivity, you must be a lifelong learner.

4. Learn how to balance your job and personal time. Realize that it is time to leave *before* you have nothing else to give physically, mentally, or emotionally.

5. You must not allow school-related stress, problem solving, and time commitments to cause you to sacrifice or neglect your family. When a career opportunity develops, discuss and get agreement that it is best for your whole family before applying for the position. If they do not feel totally comfortable with you applying, don't.

6. Faculty and staff are important keys to school success. Your role is to facilitate healthy teaching and learning. Remember, "When Mama's not happy, nobody's happy!" Well, your teachers are the Mamas of their classrooms! Work to develop and maintain a positive school culture and climate that values their input and work.

7. Be proactive. Always think ahead to possible outcomes of every decision you make. Solve problems before they develop.

8. Always have food for others in your office and at meetings. It's best if it is chocolate.

9. Don't be afraid to ask for help. Solicit advice before little problems turn into volcanoes with you knee-deep in red, hot lava.

10. Get and keep a mentor while also nurturing others through the Induction Partnership Model.

WHAT NOW?

We have spent a great deal of time together in this book studying what the Induction Partnership Model is, who can be involved with it and their roles and responsibilities, and how to use and assess it. We have talked about all seven of the Educational Leadership Constituent Council standards, what they mean in practical application, and how to correlate and align them with this induction model.

From now on, the choice is yours. You can say, "Oh, that Induction Partnership Model sounds like a really good idea," then put it away and do absolutely nothing. But what good will that do for you, for schools, for society, or for the future? Without personal involvement, an investment of time and commitment, and a structured plan for administrator development, we are going to continue getting what we already have. We will continue to have high turnover among teachers who do not have administrators prepared to provide them the support they need through their own induction process. We will continue to lose skilled and experienced teachers who are tired, frustrated, burned out, or want to earn more money for their efforts. We will continue to have new and veteran administrators who struggle with the same issues of doing what is right to make schools better while also surviving the political wars and moral dilemmas that go hand in hand with any kind of organizational leadership.

Or you can make a different choice. You can stop right now and think about everything you have read and reflected on. You can decide to make a difference with this commonsense Induction Partnership plan. You can start by selecting one new administrator and saying, "Hey, I've walked in your shoes and know it can be a very lonely place. How about if we sit down with a cup of coffee and just talk a little bit?" Sometimes it helps to have someone who has "been there and done that" to listen and commiserate with you. That's a nice opening that won't offend anyone. Assuming it works, you can cultivate the relationship and from there bring up the idea of the whole Induction Partnership Model.

Do not say, "I can't do that. I don't feel comfortable doing that." Well, life isn't always comfortable. Pick something else to say. But say something to get the process moving to support and nurture a new administrator while, at the same time, developing and honing your own professional skills.

Some people say they don't mentor because they don't have time. My question back to them is, "Do we have time *not* to mentor others? What are the consequences if we don't?" New, potentially good administrators and teachers will continue to get frustrated and leave the field. That is not a good thing. We need more good people coming in, not more good people leaving. Others say they don't mentor because, if done right, it can be time-consuming and emotionally exhausting and that working with just one mentee will not have a significant impact on the world. In other words, they are saying that helping one person to do better, cope better, lead better is just not worth it. This is the same as saying that the entire school the person works with is not worth it. Who would want to admit to something like that?

Mother Theresa had the perfect response to the importance of making a difference in the life of a single individual. She said every wonderful thing that has ever happened on earth started with just one person. You can be that one person. You can make a difference in our world by making the decision right now to become a mentor or get a mentor. Either way you will win.

I hope you have enjoyed reading, studying, and becoming a part of *Principal Induction: A Standards-Based Model for Administrator Development.* I sincerely hope it will make a difference in your life and the lives of those around you. There is no cause greater than helping others. There are people in the field of education right now who are struggling and alone. Maybe you are one of them. Get together with friends and talk to them about this induction model. Create a team to help someone else. If you are a new administrator and a seasoned veteran does not volunteer to nurture and support you, then keep your eyes open. Watch and assess the best of the best administrators around you. Then buy them a copy of this book, tell them about it, and ask them to read it. After they do so, ask them if they would be willing to help create and lead a partnership team to help you survive, grow, and become the professional you want to be. Now, who on earth could turn down a request like that? Not me, and certainly not anyone I know that values the future of our society.

To that end, I sincerely hope your lives will be filled with peace and joy. May each of your days be filled with sunshine and not rain. May you always be warm and never be hungry. May your families always be safe. And may all these things be true for every child we serve.

Suggested Readings

This list is a source of supplemental reading that supports the concepts presented in the Educational Leadership Constituent Council standards. It is not intended to include every good source. Most of these include content that is relevant to more than one standard that would be helpful for administrator induction. Read, learn, and enjoy!

STANDARD 1

Bennis, W. (1989). *Why leaders can't lead*. San Francisco: Jossey-Bass.

Blanchard, K., & Bowles, S. (1998). *Gung-ho!* New York: William Morrow.

Blanchard, K., Hybels, B., & Hodges, P. (1999). *Leadership by the book: Tools to transform your workplace*. New York: William Morrow.

Bolman, L. G., & Deal, T. E. (1997). *Reframing organizations: Artistry, choice, and leadership* (2nd ed.). San Francisco: Jossey-Bass.

Bolman, L. G., & Deal, T. E. (2001). *Leading with soul: An uncommon journey of spirit*. San Francisco: Jossey-Bass.

Brock, B. L., & Grady, M. L. (2000). *Rekindling the flame*. Thousand Oaks, CA: Corwin Press.

De Pree, M. (1989). *Leadership is an art*. New York: Dell.

DeWitt Wallace–Reader's Digest Fund Study Conference. (1992). *Developing a framework for the continual professional development of administrators in the northeast*. (ERIC Document Reproduction Service No. ED383104)

Fullan, M. (2001). *Leading in a culture of change*. San Francisco: Jossey-Bass.

Hoyle, J. (1995). *Leadership and futuring: Making visions happen*. Thousand Oaks, CA: Corwin Press.

Hoyle, J. (2001). *Leadership and the force of love: Six keys to motivating with love*. Thousand Oaks, CA: Corwin Press.

Johnson, S. (1998). *Who moved my cheese?* New York: Putnam.

Kouzes, J. M., & Posner, B. Z. (1998). *Encouraging the heart: A leader's guide to rewarding and recognizing others*. San Francisco: Jossey-Bass.

Krzyzewski, M., & Phillips, D. T. (2000). *Leading with the heart: Coach K's successful strategies for basketball, business, and life*. New York: Warner Business Books.

Maxwell, J. C. (1995). *Developing the leaders around you*. Nashville, TN: Thomas Nelson.

Peters, T., & Waterman, R. H. (1993). *In search of excellence.* New York: Warner Books.

Ramsey, R. D. (1999). *Lead, follow, or get out of the way.* Thousand Oaks, CA: Corwin Press.

Sergiovanni, T. J. (2001). *The principalship: A reflective practice perspective* (4th ed.). Needham Heights, MA: Allyn & Bacon.

STANDARD 2

Banks, J. A., & Banks, C. M. (1996). *Multicultural education: Issues and perspectives.* Boston: Allyn & Bacon.

Barker, C. L., & Searchwell, C. J. (1998). *Writing meaningful teacher evaluations—right now!!* Thousand Oaks, CA: Corwin Press.

Barker, C. L., & Searchwell, C. J. (2001). *Writing year-end teacher improvement plans—right now!!* Thousand Oaks, CA: Corwin Press.

Beach, D. M., & Reinhartz, J. (2000). *Supervisory leadership.* Boston: Allyn & Bacon.

Beane, J. A. (1997). *Curriculum integration: Designing the core of democratic education.* New York: Teachers College Press.

Bigge, M. L., & Shermis, S. S. (1999). *Learning theories for teachers* (6th ed.). New York: Addison-Wesley Longman.

Blanchard, K., & Johnson, S. (1981). *The one minute manager.* New York: Berkley.

Blase, J., & Kirby, P. C. (1992). *Bringing out the best in teachers: What effective principals do.* Thousand Oaks, CA: Corwin Press.

Bocchino, R. (1999). *Emotional literacy: To be a different kind of smart.* Thousand Oaks, CA: Corwin Press.

Bolman, L., & Deal, T. (1995). *Path to school leadership.* Thousand Oaks, CA: Corwin Press.

Bracey, G. W. (2000). *Bail me out! Handling difficult data and tough questions about public schools.* Thousand Oaks, CA: Corwin Press.

Brewer, E. W., DeJonge, J. O., & Stout, V. J. (2001). *Moving online: Making the transition from traditional instruction and communication strategies.* Thousand Oaks, CA: Corwin Press.

Bucher, R. D. (2000). *Diversity consciousness: Opening our minds to people, cultures, and opportunities.* Upper Saddle River, NJ: Prentice Hall.

Burrello, L. C., Lashley, C., & Beatty, E. E. (2001). *Educating all students together: How school leaders create unified systems.* Thousand Oaks, CA: Corwin Press.

Burton, V. R. (2000). *Rich minds, rich rewards.* Dallas, TX: Pearl.

Carbo, M. (2000). *What every principal should know about teaching reading.* Syosset, NY: National Reading Styles Institute.

Costa, A. L., & Garmston, R. J. (1994). *Cognitive coaching.* Norwood, MA: Christopher Gordon.

Creighton, T. B. (2000). *The educator's guide for using data to improve decision making.* Thousand Oaks, CA: Corwin Press.

Crow, G. M., & Matthews, L. J. (1998). *Finding one's way: How mentoring can lead to dynamic leadership.* Thousand Oaks, CA: Corwin Press.

Danielson, C., & McGreal, T. L. (2000). *Teacher evaluation to enhance professional practice.* Princeton, NJ: Educational Testing Service.

Daresh, J. (2001). *Leaders helping leaders: A practical guide to administrative mentoring* (2nd ed.). Thousand Oaks, CA: Corwin Press.

Deal, T. E., & Peterson, K. D. (1994). *The leadership paradox.* San Francisco: Jossey-Bass.

Deal, T. E., & Peterson, K. D. (1999). *Shaping school culture: The heart of leadership.* San Francisco: Jossey-Bass.

English, F. W. (2000). *Deciding what to teach and test: Developing, aligning, and auditing the curriculum* (millennium ed.). Thousand Oaks, CA: Corwin Press.

Glanz, J. (1998). *Action research: An educational guide to school improvement.* Norwood, MA: Christopher Gordan.

Glatthorn, A. A. (2001). *The principal as curriculum leader* (2nd ed.). Thousand Oaks, CA: Corwin Press.

Glenn, H. S., & Brock, M. L. (1998). *7 strategies for developing capable students.* Roseville, CA: Prima.

Gregory, G. H., & Chapman, C. (2001). *Differentiated instructional strategies: One size doesn't fit all.* Thousand Oaks, CA: Corwin Press.

Hadaway, N., Vardell, S. M., & Young, T. (2001). *Literature-based instruction with English language learners.* Boston: Allyn & Bacon.

Holcomb, E. L. (1998). *Getting excited about data: How to combine people, passion, and proof.* Thousand Oaks, CA: Corwin Press.

Hoyle, J. H., English, F., & Steffy, B. (1998). *Skills for successful 21st century school leaders.* Arlington, VA: American Association of School Administrators.

Joyce, B., & Weil, M. (1996). *Models of teaching.* Needham Heights, MA: Simon & Schuster.

Kozol, J. (1992). *Savage inequalities: Children in America's schools.* New York: Harper Perennial Library.

Kozol, J. (2000). *Ordinary resurrections: Children in the years of hope.* New York: Crown.

Leithwood, K., Aitken, R., & Jantzi, D. (2001). *Making schools smarter: A system for monitoring school and district progress* (2nd ed.). Thousand Oaks, CA: Corwin Press.

Oliva, P. F. (1997). *Supervision in today's schools* (5th ed.). New York: John Wiley.

Payne, R. K. (1998). *A framework for understanding poverty.* Baytown, TX: RFT.

Pratt, D. (1994). *Curriculum planning: A handbook for professionals:* Ft. Worth, TX: Harcourt Brace College.

Reksten, L. E. (2000). *Using technology to increase student learning.* Thousand Oaks, CA: Corwin Press.

Schlechty, P. C. (2001). *Shaking up the school house.* San Francisco: Jossey-Bass.

Sergiovanni, T. J., & Starratt, R. J. (1998). *Supervision: A redefinition* (6th ed.). Boston: McGraw-Hill.

Thompson, S. J., Quenemoen, R. F., Thurlow, M. L., & Ysseldyke, J. E. (2001). *Alternate assessments for students with disabilities.* Thousand Oaks, CA: Corwin Press.

Thurlow, M. L., Elliott, J. L., & Ysseldyke, J. E. (1998). *Testing students with disabilities: Practical strategies for complying with district and state requirements.* Thousand Oaks, CA: Corwin Press.

Weil, J., Weil, B., & Weil, M. (1998). *Models of teaching* (6th ed.). Needham Neights, MA: Simon & Schuster.

Whitaker, T. (1999). *Dealing with difficult teachers.* Larchmont, NY: Eye on Education.

Wilmore, E. L. (2002). *Principal leadership: Applying the new Educational Leadership Constituent Council Standards.* Thousand Oaks, CA: Corwin Press.

Woodward, J., & Cuban, L. (Eds.). (2001). *Technology, curriculum, and professional development: Adapting schools to meet the needs of students with disabilities.* Thousand Oaks, CA: Corwin Press.

Worthen, B., Sanders, J., & Fitzpatrick, J. (1996). *Program evaluation, alternative approaches and practical guidelines* (2nd ed.). New York: Addison-Wesley.

STANDARD 3

Anderson, J. W. (2001). *The answers to questions that teachers most frequently ask.* Thousand Oaks, CA: Corwin Press.

Bennis, W. (1997). *Managing people is like herding cats.* Provo, UT: Executive Excellence.

Brewer, E. W., Achilles, C. M., Fuhriman, J. R., & Hollingsworth, C. (2001). *Finding funding: Grantwriting from start to finish, including project management and Internet use.* Thousand Oaks, CA: Corwin Press.

Burrup, P. E., Brimpley, V., Jr., & Garfield, R. R. (1998). *Financing education in a climate of change* (7th ed.). Boston: Allyn & Bacon.

Coleman, M., & Anderson, L. (2000). *Managing finance and resources in education.* Thousand Oaks, CA: Corwin Press.

DiGiulio, R. C. (2001). *Educate, medicate, or litigate? What teachers, parents, and administrators must do about student behavior.* Thousand Oaks, CA: Corwin Press.

Dyer, K. M. (2000). *The intuitive principal.* Thousand Oaks, CA: Corwin Press.

Erlandson, D. A., Stark, P. L., & Ward, S. M. (1996). *Organizational oversight: Planning and scheduling for effectiveness.* Larchmont, NY: Eye on Education.

Fitzwater, I. (1996). *Time management for school administrators.* Rockport, MA: Pro>Active.

Ledeen, M. A. (1999). *Machiavelli on modern leadership.* New York: St. Martin's Press.

Lunenburg, F. C., & Ornstein, A. C. (2000). *Educational administration: Concepts and practices* (3rd ed.). Belmont, CA: Wadsworth/Thomas Learning.

McNamara, J. F., Erlandson, D. A., & McNamara, M. (1999). *Measurement and evaluation: Strategies for school improvement.* Larchmont, NY: Eye on Education.

Odden, A., & Archibald, S. (2001). *Reallocating resources: How to boost student achievement without asking for more.* Thousand Oaks, CA: Corwin Press.

Parsons, B. A. (2001). *Evaluative inquiry: Using evaluation to promote student success.* Thousand Oaks, CA: Corwin Press.

Peterson, S. (2001). *The grantwriter's Internet companion: A resource for educators and others seeking grants and funding.* Thousand Oaks, CA: Corwin Press.

Ramsey, R. D. (2001). *Fiscal fitness for school administrators: How to stretch resources and do even more with less.* Thousand Oaks, CA: Corwin Press.

Sanders, J. R. (2000). *Evaluating school programs* (2nd ed.). Thousand Oaks, CA: Corwin Press.

Schmieder, J. H., & Cairns, D. (1996). *Ten skills of highly effective principals.* Lancaster, PA: Technomic.

Sergiovanni, T. J. (2000). *The lifeworld of leadership.* San Francisco: Jossey-Bass.

Slavin, R. E., & Fashola, O. S. (1998). *Show me the evidence! Proven and promising programs for America's schools.* Thousand Oaks, CA: Corwin Press.

Smith, H. W. (1994). *The 10 natural laws of successful time and life management.* New York: Warner Books.

STANDARD 4

Batey, C. S. (1996). *Parents are lifesavers: A handbook for parent involvement in schools.* Thousand Oaks, CA: Corwin Press.

Bennis, W. (1999). *Old dogs, new tricks.* Provo, UT: Executive Excellence.

Burke, M. A., & Picus, L. O. (2001). *Developing community-empowered schools.* Thousand Oaks, CA: Corwin Press.

De Pree, M. (1997). *Leading without power: Finding hope in serving community.* San Francisco: Jossey-Bass.

Decker, R. H. (1997). *When a crisis hits: Will your school be ready?* Thousand Oaks, CA: Corwin Press.

Doyle, D. P., & Pimentel, S. (1999). *Raising the standard: An eight-step action guide for schools and communities.* Thousand Oaks, CA: Corwin Press.

Drucker Foundation. (1996). *The leader of the future.* San Francisco: Jossey-Bass.

Dyer, K. M., & Carothers, J. (2000). *The intuitive principal: A guide to leadership.* Thousand Oaks, CA: Corwin Press.

Epstein, J. L., Coates, L., Salinas, K. C., Sanders, M. G., & Simon, B. S. (1997). *School, family, and community partnerships: Your handbook for action.* Thousand Oaks, CA: Corwin Press.

Holcomb, E. L. (2001). *Asking the right questions: Techniques for collaboration and school change* (2nd ed.). Thousand Oaks, CA: Corwin Press.

Jayanthi, M., & Nelson, J. S. (2001). *Savvy decision making: An administrator's guide to using focus groups in schools.* Thousand Oaks, CA: Corwin Press.

Kaser, J., Mundry, S., Stiles, K. E., & Loucks-Horsley, S. (2001). *Leading every day: 124 actions for effective leadership.* Thousand Oaks, CA: Corwin Press.

Kosmoski, G. J., & Pollack, D. R. (2000). *Managing difficult, frustrating, and hostile conversations: Strategies for savvy administrators.* Thousand Oaks, CA: Corwin Press.

McEwan, E. K. (1997). *Leading your team to excellence: How to make quality decisions.* Thousand Oaks, CA: Corwin Press.

Seiler, T. L. (2001). *Developing your case for support.* San Francisco: Jossey-Bass.

Thomas, S. J. (1999). *Designing surveys that work! A step-by-step guide.* Thousand Oaks, CA: Corwin Press.

Trump, K. S. (1998). *Practical school security: Basic guidelines for safe and secure schools.* Thousand Oaks, CA: Corwin Press.

Veale, J. R., Morley, R. E., & Erickson, C. L. (2001). *Practical evaluation for collaborative services: Goals, processes, tools, and reporting systems for school-based programs.* Thousand Oaks, CA: Corwin Press.

Wachter, J. C. (1999). *Classroom volunteers: Uh-Oh! Or Right On!* Thousand Oaks, CA: Corwin Press.

Whitaker, T. A., Whitaker, B., & Lumpa, D. (2000). *Motivating and inspiring teachers: The educational leader's guide for building staff morale.* Larchmont, NY: Eye on Education.

STANDARD 5

Blanchard, K., Oncken, W., Jr., & Burrows, H. (1989). *The one minute manager meets the monkey.* New York: William Morrow.

Blanchard, K., & Peale, N. V. (1988). *The power of ethical management.* New York: Fawcett Columbine.

Blanchard, K., Zigarmi, P., & Zigmari, D. (1985). *Leadership and the one minute manager.* New York: William Morrow.

Dunklee, D. R. (2000). *If you want to lead, not just manage: A primer for principals.* Thousand Oaks, CA: Corwin Press.

Gray, K. C. (1999). *Getting real: Helping teens find their future.* Thousand Oaks, CA: Corwin Press.

Josephson, M. S., & Hanson, W. (1998). *The power of character.* San Francisco: Jossey-Bass.

Osier, J. L., & Fox, H. P. (2001). *Settle conflicts right now! A step-by-step guide for K-6 classrooms.* Thousand Oaks, CA: Corwin Press.

Pellicer, L. O. (1999). *Caring enough to lead: Schools and the sacred trust.* Thousand Oaks, CA: Corwin Press.

Podesta, C. (1993). *Self-esteem and the 6-second secret* (updated edition). Newbury Park, CA: Corwin Press.

Podesta, C., & Sanderson, V. (1999). *Life would be easy if it weren't for other people.* Thousand Oaks, CA: Corwin Press.

Sergiovanni, T. J. (1992). *Moral leadership: Getting to the heart of school improvement.* San Francisco: Jossey-Bass.

Snowden, P. E., & Gorton, R. A. (1998). *School leadership and administration: Important concepts, case studies, and simulations* (5th ed.). New York: McGraw-Hill.

York-Barr, J., Sommers, W. A., Ghere, G. S., & Montie, J. (2001). *Reflective practice to improve schools: An action guide for educators.* Thousand Oaks, CA: Corwin Press.

STANDARD 6

Covey, S. R. (1990a). *Principle-centered leadership.* New York: Simon & Schuster.

Covey, S. R. (1990b). *The seven habits of highly effective people.* New York: Simon & Schuster.

Covey, S. R., Merrill, A. R., & Merrill, R. R. (1994). *First things first.* New York: Simon & Schuster.

Dunklee, D. R., & Shoop, R. J. (2001). *The principal's quick-reference guide to school law: reducing liability, litigation, and other potential legal tangles.* Thousand Oaks: Corwin Press.

English, F. W. (1994). *Theory in educational administration.* New York: HarperCollins.

Hoy, W. H., & Miskel, C. G. (1996). *Educational administration: Theory, research, and practice* (5th ed.). New York: McGraw-Hill.

Palestini, R. H. (1999). *Educational administration: Leading with mind and heart.* Lancaster, PA: Technomic.

Reagan, T. G., Case, C. W., & Brubacher, J. W. (2000). *Becoming a reflective educator: How to build a culture of inquiry in the schools.* Thousand Oaks, CA: Corwin Press.

Reinhartz, J., & Beach, D. M. (2003). *Foundations of educational leadership: Changing schools, changing roles.* Boston: Allyn & Bacon.

Schumaker, D. R., & Sommers, W. A. (2001). *Being a successful principal: Riding the wave of change without drowning.* Thousand Oaks, CA: Corwin Press.

Skrla, L., Erlandson, D. A., Reed, E. M., & Wilson, A. P. (2001). *The emerging principalship.* Larchmont, NY: Eye on Education.

Sperry, D. J. (1999). *Working in a legal and regulatory environment: A handbook for school leaders.* Larchmont, NY: Eye on Education.

Streshly, W. A., Walsh, J., & Frase, L. E. (2001). *Avoiding legal hassles: What school administrators really need to know* (2nd ed.). Thousand Oaks, CA: Corwin Press.

Thomson, S. (Ed.). (1993). *Principals of our changing schools: Knowledge and skill base.* Alexandria, VA: National Policy Board for Educational Administration.

STANDARD 7

Alvy, H. B., & Robbins, P. (1998). *If I only knew . . . Success strategies for navigating the principalship.* Thousand Oaks, CA: Corwin Press.

Brown, G., & Irby, B. (2001). *The principal portfolio* (2nd ed.). Thousand Oaks, CA: Corwin Press.

Capasso, R. L., & Daresh, J. C. (2001). *The school administrator internship handbook: Leading, mentoring, and participating in the internship program.* Thousand Oaks, CA: Corwin Press.

Daresh, J. (2001). *What it means to be a principal: Your guide to leadership.* Thousand Oaks, CA: Corwin Press.

Daresh, J., & Playco, M. (2001). *Beginning the principalship: A practical guide for new school leaders* (2nd ed.). Thousand Oaks, CA: Corwin Press.

Hartzell, G. N., Williams, R. C., & Nelson, K. T. (1995). *New voices in the field: The work lives of first-year assistant principals.* Thousand Oaks, CA: Corwin Press.

Irby, B. J., & Brown, G. (2000). *The career advancement portfolio.* Thousand Oaks, CA: Corwin Press.

Robbins, P., & Alvy, H. B. (1995). *The principal's companion: Strategies and hints to make the job easier.* Thousand Oaks, CA: Corwin Press.

Sharp, W. L., Walter, J. K., & Sharp, H. M. (1998). *Case studies for school leaders: Implementing the ISLLC standards.* Lancaster, PA: Technomic.

Villani, S. (1999). *Are you sure you're the principal? On being an authentic leader.* Thousand Oaks, CA: Corwin Press.

Wyatt, R. L., III, & Looper, S. (2000). *So you have to have a portfolio: A teacher's guide to preparation and presentation.* Thousand Oaks, CA: Corwin Press.

References

Agnes, M. (Ed.). (2001). *Webster's new world college dictionary* (4th ed.). Foster City, CA: IDG Books.

Bloom, B. S. (1956). *Taxonomy of educational objectives. Handbook I: Cognitive domain.* New York: McKay.

Bloom, B. S. (1982). *Human characteristics and school learning.* New York: McGraw-Hill.

Bolman, L., & Deal, T. (2002). *Reframing the path to school leadership.* Thousand Oaks, CA: Corwin Press.

Clinton, H. R. (2003). *Recruiting teachers for our classrooms.* Retrieved March 11, 2003, from http://clinton.senate.gov/issues_education.html

Council of Chief State School Officers. (1996). *Interstate school leaders licensure consortium: Standards for school leaders.* Washington, DC: Author.

Covey, S. R. (1990a). *Principle-centered leadership.* New York: Simon & Schuster.

Covey, S. R. (1990b). *The seven habits of highly effective people.* New York: Simon & Schuster.

Edmonds, R. (1979). *A discussion of the literature and issues related to effective schooling.* (ERIC Document Reproduction Service No ED170394)

Edmonds, R. (1983). *An overview of school improvement programs.* East Lansing, MI: Institute for Research on Teaching, Michigan State University.

Erlandson, D. A., Atkinson, J. N., & Wilmore, E. (1995). *The Management Profile: A handbook for the development of leadership and management skills.* College Station, TX: Principals' Center Press.

Erlandson, D. A., Lacy, V. J., & Wilmore, E. (1990). *The Management Profile: The principalship in the 1990s and beyond: Current research on performance-based preparation and professional development* [monograph series]. Tempe, AZ: Arizona State University College of Education.

Fenwick, L. T., & Pierce, M. C. (2001). The principal shortage: Crisis or opportunity? *Principal, 80,* 24–28.

Hoyle, J. R. (2002). *Leadership and the force of love.* Thousand Oaks, CA: Corwin Press.

Keeton Strayhorn, C. (2003, January). Alleviate the Texas teacher shortage. In *Limited government, unlimited opportunity.* Retrieved March 11, 2003, from the Window on State Government Web site: www.window.state.tx.us/etexas2003/ed04.html

Maxwell, J. C. (1995). *Developing the leaders around you.* Nashville, TN: Thomas Nelson.

McCowan, C., Arnold, M., Miles, D., & Hargadine, K. (2000). Why principals succeed: Comparing principal performance to national professional standards. *ERS Spectrum, 18*(2), 14–19.

Medina, J. (2003, February 26). What it will take to recruit principals: A lot. *New York Times,* pp. 1–3. Retrieved August 20, 2003, from http://www.nytimes.com/2003/02/26/education/26PRIN.html?ex=1061524800&en=bc4ca12a8290bbf5&ei=5070

Million, J. (1998, April). Where have all the principals gone? *NAESP Communicator, 21,* 5.

Murphy, J., & Shipman, N. J. (1998). *The interstate school leaders licensure consortium: A standards-based approach to strengthening educational leadership.* Paper presented to the annual conference of the American Educational Research Association, San Diego, CA.

Murphy, J., Shipman, N. J., & Pearlman, M. (1997). Strengthening educational leadership: The ISLLC standards. *Streamlined Seminar, 16,* 1–4.

Murphy, J., Yff, J., & Shipman, N. J. (2000). Implementation of the interstate school leaders licensure consortium standards. *International Journal of Leadership in Education, 3,* 17–39.

National Association of Elementary School Principals. (n.d.). NAESP fact sheet on the principal shortage. Retrieved from http://www.naesp.org/misc/prin_shrtg_facts.htm

National Association of Secondary School Principals. (2001). The principal shortage [fact sheet]. Retrieved March 11, 2003, from http://www.principals.org/advocacy/prin_shrt.cfm

National Association of Secondary School Principals. (2002). Study confirms powerful link between the principal and school success: Shortage of qualified candidates hindering the improvement of schools. Retrieved May 5, 2002, from http://www.principals.org/advocacy/pr_shrt_qual_cndid.cfm

National Policy Board for Educational Administration. (2001). *Advanced programs in educational leadership for principals, superintendents, curriculum directors, and supervisors.* Washington, DC: Author.

Portner, H. (2002). *Being mentored: A guide for protégés.* Thousand Oaks, CA: Corwin Press.

Potter, L. (2001). Solving the principal shortage. *Principal, 80,* 34–37.

Richardson, L. (1999, June 23). Principal: A tougher job, fewer takers. *The Los Angeles Times,* p. A1.

Schnur, J.(2002, June 18). *An outstanding principal in every school: Using the new title II to promote effective leadership.* Retrieved August 12, 2003, from the National Council on Teacher Quality Web site: http://www.nctq.org/press/2002_consumers_guide/schnur.html

Snyder, W. (2001). *The quality of worklife in K–12 public education: A limiting factor in attracting, recruiting, developing and retaining quality teachers and school executives.* Retrieved March 14, 2003, from the White Papers Web site of Florida State University: http://www.coe.fsu.edu/whitepapers/quality.htm

Study warns of shortage of qualified candidates for principalship. (1998, May). *Copy Editor, 55,* 1.

Thomson, S. (Ed.). (1993). *Principals of our changing schools: Knowledge and skill base.* Alexandria, VA: National Policy Board for Educational Administration.

U.S. Bureau of Labor Statistics. *Education Administrators.* (2000–2001). *Occupational outlook handbook.* Retrieved November 26, 2001, from http://www.bls.gov/ oco/

U.S. Department of Education. (2002). *A quality teacher in every classroom: Improving teacher quality and enhancing the profession.* Retrieved May 31, 2002, from the U.S. Department of Education Web site: http://ed.gov.whitehouse.gov/infocus/education/teachers/quality_teachers.html

Van Meter, E., & Murphy, J. (1997). *Using ISLLC standards to strengthen preparation programs in school administration.* Washington, DC: Council of Chief State School Officers.

Whitehurst, G. (2002). *Research on teacher preparation and professional development.* Retrieved May 31, 2002, from the U.S. Department of Education Web site: http://www/ed/gov/inits/preparingteachersconference/poloakloff.html

Wilmore, E. (1988). The establishment of criteria for standards of principal performance. (Doctoral dissertation, Texas A&M University, 1988). *Dissertation Abstracts International, 50/04-A,* 850 (University Microfilms No. AAD89–13473).

Wilmore, E. (1992). The Management Profile: The identification of management and leadership skills of school administrators. *The Instructional Leader, V*(1), 4–7, 12.

Wilmore, E. (1993). The Management Profile and site-based management: An idea whose time has come. *The NASSP Bulletin, 77*(550), 84–88.

Wilmore, E. (1999). Where there's a will there's a way: Creating university, public, private, and charter school collaboratives. *Education, 119*(3).

Wilmore, E. (2000). The changing role of school leadership preparation. *International Journal of Educational Reform, 9,* 349–359.

Wilmore, E. L. (2001). *Passing the principal ExCet exam: How to get certified the first time.* Thousand Oaks, CA: Corwin Press.

Wilmore, E., & Atkinson, N. J. (1993). The management profile: Identification of the management and leadership skills of school administrators. *Journal of School Leadership, 3,* 566–578.

Wilmore, E., & Erlandson, D. A. (1993). Planning for professional growth: A process for administrators. *The NASSP Bulletin, 77*(551), 57–63.

Wilmore, E., & McNeil, J. J., Jr. (1999). Who will lead our schools? *International Journal of Educational Reform, 8,* 365–373.

Wilmore, E., & Thomas, C. (1998). Authentic administrative preparation: Linking theory to practice. *International Journal of Educational Reform, 7,* 172–177.

Wise, A. E. (2002, June 13). *On the U.S. Department of Education report on teacher quality "Meeting the Highly Qualified Teachers Challenge."* Retrieved March 13, 2003, from the National Council for Accreditation of Teacher Education Web site: http://www.ncate.org/newsbrfs/hqt_602.htm

Index

**CORWIN
PRESS**

The Corwin Press logo—a raven striding across an open book—represents the union of courage and learning. Corwin Press is committed to improving education for all learners by publishing books and other professional development resources for those serving the field of K–12 education. By providing practical, hands-on materials, Corwin Press continues to carry out the promise of its motto: **"Helping Educators Do Their Work Better**."